P9-CEG-761

OVERCOMING DEPRESSION

DR. NEIL T. AND JOANNE ANDERSON

Regal

From Gospel Light
Ventura, California, U.S.A.

Published by Regal Books
From Gospel Light
Ventura, California, U.S.A.
Printed in the U.S.A.

Regal Books is a ministry of Gospel Light, a Christian publisher dedicated to serving the local church. We believe God's vision for Gospel Light is to provide church leaders with biblical, user-friendly materials that will help them evangelize, disciple and minister to children, youth and families.

It is our prayer that this Regal book will help you discover biblical truth for your own life and help you meet the needs of others. May God richly bless you.

For a free catalog of resources from Regal Books/Gospel Light, please call your Christian supplier or contact us at 1-800-4-GOSPEL or www.regalbooks.com.

Cover design by David Griffing
Edited by Amy Spence.

Library of Congress Cataloging-in-Publication Data

Anderson, Neil T., 1942–
  Overcoming depression / Neil T. and Joanne Anderson.
    p. cm.
  ISBN 0-8307-3351-5
  1. Depression, Mental—Religious aspects—Christianity. 2. Depressed persons—Religious life. I. Anderson, Joanne, 1941- II. Title.
  BV4910.34.A535 2004
  248.8'625–dc22   2004002084

1 2 3 4 5 6 7 8 9 10 11 12 13 14 15 10 09 08 07 06 05

Rights for publishing this book in other languages are contracted by Gospel Light Worldwide, the international nonprofit ministry of Gospel Light. Gospel Light Worldwide also provides publishing and technical assistance to international publishers dedicated to producing Sunday School and Vacation Bible School curricula and books in the languages of the world. For additional information, visit www.gospellightworldwide.org; write to Gospel Light Worldwide, P.O. Box 3875, Ventura, CA 93006; or send an e-mail to info@gospellightworldwide.org.

CONTENTS

ACKNOWLEDGMENTS

So many people have contributed to this book. Chief among them have been those who have suffered the most. Every attempt we have made to minister to them has been a learning experience. About the time we think we have heard it all, along comes another case that adds to the complexity of the problem. The valleys are where we all grow and where we change the direction of our lives. Joanne's struggle with depression changed our lives for the better and was the primary event that precipitated the founding of Freedom in Christ Ministries.

We want to thank Hal Baumchen for his contribution to our first book on depression, *Finding Hope Again* (Regal Books, 2000). This book is a compilation of Neil's part in that first book along with Joanne's insights as a survivor of depression. We also want to thank Dr. Stephen and Judy King for their contribution. Stephen is a psychiatrist and serves on the board of Freedom in Christ Ministries. He is our primary source for information on the proper use of medication. Judy is a therapist who has taught an elective on depression at Living Free in Christ conferences, and she is a coauthor of *Released from Bondage* (Thomas Nelson, 2002) with Neil and Dr. Fernando Garzon.

Finally, we want to thank Gospel Light for making this book a part of the Victory over the Darkness series. Gospel Light is our partner in helping people discover who they are in Christ and how to live a liberated life in Him.

INTRODUCTION

Joanne informed me that Mary was in the hospital again. This was the third time that she was admitted for clinical depression. Joanne had an opportunity to pray for Mary at the hospital and discuss her situation. Mary had dutifully followed her doctor's orders and had tried every scientific remedy known, to no avail. Somewhat apologetically, Joanne suggested, "Why don't you go see Neil?" "Him!" she responded incredulously. "How could he help me? He's always up!"

Isn't that the kind of person from whom she should seek help? If you were really feeling sick, would you seek out a sickly, emaciated, wasted doctor and ask what his or her health secret is? Surely if you were down, you would want to see or at least learn from someone who is "always up." That kind of person must be doing or believing something that enables him or her to live above his or her circumstances. From Mary's perspective, however, I don't think that was the primary issue. She was probably thinking:

> *How could someone who is "always up" understand what I am going through? Do you know what it is like to get up every morning with no sense of hope and not enough energy to climb out of bed? Negative thoughts pepper my mind, and I'm emotionally drained all the time. I may have a few good moments, but they never last. I can't even muster enough energy to think properly. The slightest little irritation sets off another round of despair. One more bad report and I'll be ready to cash it in. I can't take it anymore. I don't have the strength or the will to fight. I just want to curl up in a ball and die. It seems like the only way out, and my family would be better off if I did die.*

Such are the negative, repeating, oppressive thoughts of the melancholic. It is bad enough to suffer from such a malady, but to endure the stares, rejection or pious platitudes of those who don't understand is to add insult to injury. There was a time when Neil's natural bent would be to "jolly up" such a person. Then Joanne read to him from the Bible, "He who blesses his friend with a loud voice early in the morning, it will be reckoned a curse to him" (Prov. 27:14). A little comic relief can be a shaft of light in a dark world, but it usually doesn't last, nor does it resolve the cause for the depression.

If a depressed person doesn't believe that a joyful mortal can relate to his or her circumstances or understand what he or she is going through, then how can the person expect God to understand? After all, if He doesn't like the present circumstances, He can create new ones. God doesn't have to deal with our finite limitations; He is eternal and infinite. He has no impure thoughts, nor does He struggle with insurmountable odds.

JESUS CAN RELATE

The statement, "God can relate," may not seem true if you only knew Him as your heavenly Father, but remember Jesus. He humbled Himself and took on the form of a man. He voluntarily surrendered the independent use of His divine attributes. All the political and religious forces were united against Him. In the end, He was all alone. Even His chosen disciples deserted Him. Peter denied that he even knew Him. In the garden of Gethsemane, Jesus was grieved and distressed to the point of death. He was the man of sorrows acquainted with grief. Finally, He faced the mockery of a trial and was found guilty of trumped-up charges. Jesus, the most innocent man who ever lived, was crucified. According to Hebrews 4:14-16, we can go to God because of Jesus:

> Since we have a great high priest who has passed through the heavens, Jesus the Son of God, let us hold fast our confession. For we do not have a high priest who cannot sympathize with our weaknesses, but One who has been tempted in all things as we are, yet without sin. Therefore let us draw near with confidence to the throne of grace, so that we may receive mercy and find grace to help in time of need.

Jesus made it possible for us to go to God not only because He died for our sins and gave us eternal life but also because He, by His own experience, can relate to our weaknesses. He knows from personal experience how we feel. Have you ever felt rejected and unloved? So has He. Have you ever had people you counted on let you down? So has He. Do you face overwhelming temptation? He was tempted in *all* ways. Do you have to live with the consequences of someone else's sins? He took upon Himself the sins of *all* humankind and then faced what you and I will never have to face—the Father turning His back on Him. We can say with confidence, "God will never leave us nor forsake us" (see Deut. 31:6). In spite of all that He endured, Jesus never lost hope or faith in the heavenly Father. The resources that sustained Him are now ours in Christ. He is the God of all hope.

WE RECEIVE MERCY AND GRACE

We have the assurance that if we go to God, we will receive mercy and find grace to help in time of need. He will not give us what we deserve (which demonstrates His mercy); instead, He will give us what we need (which demonstrates His grace), even though we don't deserve it. People don't always see the Church as a house of mercy. In too many cases, they receive more mercy and less judgment in a secular treatment center or local bar. However, those places don't have the eternal grace of God to help in times of need. In Christ we have that grace to help, but we won't have the opportunity to share it if we don't first show mercy. The cry of the depressed is, *Have mercy upon me. I don't need to be scolded, judged, advised or rejected. I need to be understood, accepted, affirmed and loved.* If that doesn't come first, then all the biblical answers we have to give them will fall upon deaf ears.

WE MUST NOT HIDE

Determining the causes and cures of depression presents a challenge, because the symptoms reveal that the whole person—body, soul and spirit—is affected. We know that many people are physically sick for psychosomatic reasons.[1] We also know that many physically sick people suffer emotionally. Humanly speaking, we hope a physical cause and cure can be found for depression since there is less social stigma associated with a physical illness than a mental illness. We feel somehow absolved of our responsibility if a physical cause can be established. Our sense of worth is left intact. We believe others will be more sympathetic if they know our depression isn't our fault.

With that kind of thinking, people are afraid to share their emotional problems. Tremendous needs go unmet when people share only their physical problems but not their emotional or spiritual ones. Generally speaking, the Christian community doesn't know how to respond to those who struggle emotionally. On the other hand, if people break their legs, we flock to the hospital, pray for them and sign their casts. We bring meals to people's homes. We treat them almost like heroes, because we understand physical illnesses and we can sympathize.

Consider what happens, however, when a prayer request is given by someone who is depressed. A gloom hangs over the room and a polite prayer is offered: "Dear Lord, help Mary get over her depression. Amen." The Christian community has not been taught how to respond to emotional problems. There is no cast to sign, and everyone is silently thinking (or the depressed believe that others are thinking), *Why doesn't she just snap out of it? I wonder what skeletons she has in her closet? If she would just pray and read her Bible more she wouldn't be in such a state. No sincere Christian should be depressed. There must be some sin in her life.* These critical thoughts are not helpful to the depressed person and often aren't true. Contributing to a person's guilt and shame does not help mental functioning. We must learn to reflect the love and hope of God who binds up the brokenhearted.

Is there a physical cause and therefore a potential physical cure for some forms of depression? Yes, and we will examine those possibilities. Christians are no more immune to endogenous (i.e., from within the body, or physical in its origin) depression than non-Christian people. Therefore, it is wrong to jump to the conclusion that it is a sin for a Christian to be depressed. We have a far greater hope, however, if the cause of our depression is *not* endogenous. Changing brain chemistry is far less certain and less precise than changing what we believe or how we think. However, it is usually easier to get a person to take a pill with the hope of changing brain chemistry than it is to get that person to change what he or she believes and how he or she thinks. If people are depressed because of the way they think and believe, then why are depressed people shunned or judged more than arrogant, prideful and self-sufficient people? The depressed person would find a more kindred spirit with the prophets in the Bible than the latter group.

A WHOLISTIC ANSWER IS REQUIRED

In one sense it doesn't make any difference whether the precipitating cause for depression is physical, mental or spiritual. Depression affects the whole person, and a complete cure requires a wholistic answer. No human problem manifesting in one dimension of reality can be isolated from the rest of reality. Like any other sickness of the body and soul, depression is a whole-life problem that requires a whole-life answer. Depression is related to our physical health, what we believe, how we perceive ourselves, our relationship with God, our relationships with others, the circumstances of life, and finally, it may have something to do with Satan, who is the god of this world. You cannot successfully treat depression without taking into account all related factors. We have a whole God who is the creator of all reality, and He relates to us as whole people.

WE ARE NOT ALONE

There is no shame in feeling depressed since depression is an inevitable part of our maturing process. Approximately 19 million people in America (about 10 percent of all adults) will suffer from depression in any given year.[2] Only one-third of those people will seek treatment for their depression. In too many cases, pride prevents us from seeking the help we need, and the consequences are often predictable and tragic. Pride comes before a fall, and God is opposed to the proud. It is more honest and liberating to admit that we need help than it is to pretend we can live the Christian life in isolation. Our drive to be self-sufficient undermines our sufficiency in Christ. Those who are secure in Christ readily admit their need for one another, and they don't hesitate to ask for help when it is necessary. We absolutely need God, and we necessarily need each other. It is the essence of love to meet the needs of others.

David was said to have a whole heart for God, yet his numerous bouts of depression are recorded throughout the Psalms. Some say Martin Luther battled depression most of his life. Abraham Lincoln said, "I am now the most miserable man living. If what I feel were equally distributed to the whole human family, there would not be one cheerful face on the earth."[3] Friends of Abraham Lincoln said, "He was a sad looking man; his melancholy dript from him as he walked,"[4] and "He was so overcome with mental depression that he never dare[d] carry a knife in his pocket."[5] Sir Winston Churchill, the prime minister of England during World War II, referred to his recurrent depression as the black dog. A biographer notes, "He had an enemy worthy of the word [black dog], an unambiguous tyrant whose destruction occupied him fully and invigorated him totally year in and year out."[6]

Let's face it, living in this fallen world can be depressing. Depression is a natural consequence when we experience losses in our lives. Therefore, it is critically important that we understand how to respond to such losses, since everything we possess we shall someday lose. It is God's intention that we grow through the trials of life and learn how to overcome feelings of helplessness and hopelessness. The richest treasures are often discovered in the deepest holes. What we need is the assurance that can come only from a God of all hope. Someone once said:

> We can live about 40 days without food, about three days without water, and about eight minutes without air—but only one second without hope.[7]

TRUTH RESTORES HOPE

We wrote this book to help you establish your hope in God and enable you to live according to the truth of God's Word. We want to extend to you the mercy and grace of God. Depression, despair and hopelessness may have crept into your life and tainted your view of reality. Yet truth restores hope. We want to help you see the reality of the world we live in through the grid of Scripture. Wisdom is seeing life from God's perspective. Neil has not struggled with deep depression, but Joanne has. We will share our story of overcoming a depression so severe that it almost destroyed us. You will read many other stories of people recovering from depression. The names have been changed for most of the stories, but some have wanted to openly share their testimonies of finding freedom in Christ. For literary sake, we have written the book using "I" and "we" without distinguishing whether the writer was Neil or Joanne. In this book, we will

1. Describe the symptoms and signs of depression in order to facilitate a proper diagnosis
2. Explain medical terminology, brain chemistry and neurological functioning so that you can understand the organic part of depression
3. Show how thinking and believing affect how we respond to the external world in which we live
4. Establish the spiritual connection to mental health
5. Reveal the Father nature of God and how He relates to us

6. Explain the gospel and establish who we are in Christ and what it means to be a child of God
7. Uncover the truth from Scripture that destroys our sense of hopelessness and helplessness
8. Help us understand how we can survive the inevitable losses of life and how any crisis can be a stepping-stone to greater maturity
9. Provide a step-by-step process for overcoming depression

Jesus prayed, "But now I come to You; and these things I speak in the world so that they may have My joy made full in themselves" (John 17:13). Paul said, "Not that we lord it over your faith, but are workers with you for your joy; for in your faith you are standing firm" (2 Cor. 1:24). God wants you to experience the joy of the Lord. Joy is a fruit of the Spirit (see Gal. 5:22-23), not a fruit of circumstances. We are workers with you for your joy. However, the Christian walk is not about trying to be happy—that would be trite, misguided and self-serving.

Rather, you are called to be a mission-minded overcomer in Christ. To continuously live a beaten-down, defeated life in bondage is not your calling. To see yourself as rejected, unwanted and useless is to be deceived. To see the circumstances of life as hopeless is to take your eyes off Jesus, the author and finisher of your faith. To think you are unloved, unappreciated and unworthy is to believe a lie, because you are a child of the King who has rescued you from the domain of darkness and transferred you to the Kingdom of His beloved Son (see Col. 1:13). God's love for you is unconditional, because God *is* love. It is His nature to love you.

Our prayer is that you will sense our compassion and understanding derived from years of helping people who have lost their hope. Our compassion and understanding are imperfect, but God's love and compassion are not. He is your hope. We have chosen to speak the truth in love but to be tender enough to bind up the brokenhearted. We believe in the personal presence of Christ in your life, and the truth of His Word is the ultimate answer. Our desire is to make that truth relevant to your struggles and practical enough to inspire immediate action.

Now may the God of hope fill you with all joy and peace in believing, so that you will abound in hope by the power of the Holy Spirit.

ROMANS 15:13

DIAGNOSING DEPRESSION

The signs of approaching melancholy are . . . anguish and distress, dejections, silence, animosity . . . sometimes a desire to live and at other times a longing for death, suspicions on the part of the patient that a plot is being hatched against him.

CAELIUS AURELIANUS, HEALER
(METHODIST SCHOOL OF MEDICINE),
A.D. FIFTH CENTURY

A pastor and his wife began their session in tears. Their son had been killed in an automobile accident nine days earlier. They had been through hard times before and were intimately acquainted with sorrow and grief. They reminisced about their son as we talked and prayed together. Being in ministry, they knew of God's grace and comfort. The pastor and his wife had helped many others work through their crises, but now he was despondent and unable to sleep. The loss was overwhelming to him.

Another man, Steven, had been unemployed for almost 20 weeks following a minor accident with his semitruck. No one had been injured, but his company suspended him from driving, and he quit out of embarrassment and shame. He had been unable to explore new employment possibilities and made up stories for my sake about the "activities" that he used to occupy his time. He felt helpless and hopeless. He was hesitant to talk about the future.

A woman in her 30s was deeply troubled and physically shook during our meeting. A single parent of a nine-year-old child, she worked in a nursing home and was going to school at night. Although she had long ago left her parents, she talked of the ongoing strain and tension in their relationship. She reflected on her spiritual life and the terrible condition of her soul. With trembling voice and frightened eyes, she said she had committed the unpardonable sin. The "voices" in her mind harassed her at every turn. They called her "slut" and "nasty" and told her that Jesus would never talk to her again after what she had done. She was extremely agitated and anxious.

A Sad Epidemic

These stories of loss, hopelessness and spiritual defeat seem so different and unrelated, yet each person's diagnosis was depression. Depression is an ache in the soul that crushes the spirit. It wraps itself so tightly around you that you can't believe that it will ever leave, but it can and it does! Depression is treatable. You do not have to live like this, at least not for long.

About 10 million people in America are presently suffering from depression. It creeps into the lives of all people regardless of age, sex, social status or economic status. Twice as many women struggle with depression as do men. Twenty-five percent of college students struggle with some form of depression, and

> DEPRESSION IS AN ACHE
> IN THE SOUL THAT CRUSHES
> THE SPIRIT. YOU DO NOT
> HAVE TO LIVE LIKE THIS.

33 percent of college dropouts will suffer serious depression before leaving school. The number of doctor visits in which patients received prescriptions for mental problems rose from 32.7 million to 45.6 million during the decade from 1985 to 1994. Visits in which depression was diagnosed almost doubled over those 10 years from 11 million to more than 20.4 million.[1] This is an incredible increase in 10 years, especially in light of the fact that many who struggle with depression do not seek medical help.

Depression is a complex yet common physical, emotional and spiritual struggle. It is so prevalent that it has been called the common cold of mental illness. Many people will have at least one serious bout of depression in their lifetime, and every person will experience some symptoms of depression due to poor physical health, negative circumstances or weak spiritual condition. Too many Christians live in denial about their own depression thinking that if they were spiritually mature, then they would never have to struggle like the rest of us. Consequently, they don't reach out to others or seek the help they need. It is actually shameful in some "Christian" communities to be sad or depressed. *You must be living in sin* is the deceptive assumption. Such erroneous or simplistic thinking causes people to hide their true feelings instead of believing the truth and walking in the light.

SIGNS OF DEPRESSION

Depression is a disturbance or disorder of one's mood or emotional state. It is characterized by persistent sadness, heaviness, darkness or feelings of emptiness. The emotional state of depression is usually accompanied by thoughts of hopelessness and sometimes suicide. Depressed people believe that life is bad and the prognosis of improvement is nil. Their thoughts are colored by negative and pessimistic views of themselves, their future and their surrounding circumstances.

It is critically important to realize that the *emotional state* of depression is not the cause, it is the symptom. Treating the symptom only brings temporary relief at best. Any treatment for depression must focus on the cause, not the effect. The goal is to cure the disease, not the resulting pain. As we will examine later, the cause can be physical, mental or spiritual. We think it is important to understand the symptoms of depression in order to better understand the cause. A proper diagnosis is necessary before appropriate treatment can be considered.

PHYSICAL SYMPTOMS OF DEPRESSION

Energy Level: *I just don't feel like doing anything.*
Loss of energy, excessive fatigue and unrelenting tiredness are the characteristics of the melancholic. Walking, talking, cleaning the house, getting ready for work or doing a project can

take a considerably longer time than usual. The person suffering from depression also feels that time is moving at a snail's pace and usual activities become monumental or seemingly insurmountable tasks. Fatigue and tiredness are common complaints. The lowered energy level and lowered interest in activities affect job performance. The depressed person knows his or her performance is sliding but can't seem to pull out of the depression.

Approximately 10 percent of the melancholic seriously struggle with endogenous (i.e., from within the body, or physical in its origin) depression. Many of them simply do not function on a daily basis. They don't get dressed and either stay in bed or lie around the house. They cease to function in life.

Sleep Disturbance: *I didn't sleep again last night!*

Having trouble sleeping is one of the most common symptoms of depression. Although some people feel like sleeping all of the time, insomnia is actually more common. Initial insomnia (sleep-onset insomnia) is difficulty in falling asleep. Depression is more commonly associated with terminal insomnia—falling asleep out of sheer fatigue but then waking up, unable to get back to sleep. The inability to sleep is a symptom of depression, but it also contributes to the downward spiral of those who can't seem to pull out of the depression. Inadequate sleep leaves the sufferer with less energy for tomorrow.

Psalm 77 is a call for help by someone who begins his lament by questioning God (see vv. 7-9). In such a state, he writes, "When I remember God, then I am disturbed; when I sigh, then my spirit grows faint. You have held my eyelids open; I am so troubled that I cannot speak" (vv. 3-4). His hope is gone because what he believes about God is not true, and the result is sleeplessness and not enough energy to even speak. That is depression.

Activity Level: *Why bother!*

Depression is accompanied by a decreased involvement in meaningful activities and a lack of interest in life and commitment to follow through. Sufferers don't have the physical or emotional energy to sustain their ordinary levels of activity, and their performance is often hindered. Many find it difficult to pray because God seems distant. Perhaps they used to enjoy playing the piano or some other instrument, but they no longer find it relaxing or satisfying. Tragically, the need for self-expression and to be involved in a community goes unmet, which contributes to their depression.

Lack of Sex Drive: *Not tonight!*

In depression there is often a decrease in sexual interest, or drive. Accompanying this loss of desire for sex is a wish for isolation, feelings of worthlessness, criticism of one's own appearance, loss of spontaneity, and apathy. The emotional state of depression usually creates problems in relationships, which obviously further curtails the desire to be intimate.

Somatic Complaint: *I ache all over!*

Many depressed people report physical aches and pains such as headaches, stomachaches and lower-back pain, which can be quite severe. Depression headaches are often present. Unlike migraine headaches, they are dull and feel like a band around the head with pain radiating down the neck. In a state of depression, David wrote, "I am bowed down and brought very low; all day long I go about mourning. My back is filled with searing pain; there is no health in my body" (Ps. 38:6-7, *NIV*).

Loss of Appetite: *I'm not hungry!*

Depression is often accompanied by a decrease in appetite. Indigestion, constipation or diarrhea contribute to weight loss during depression. Those who struggle with anorexia are usually depressed as well. However, in 20 percent of depression cases, there is an increase of appetite and craving for food.

MENTAL AND EMOTIONAL SYMPTOMS OF DEPRESSION

The most noticeable symptoms of depression are emotional. There are also resultant mental states that indicate severe to mild depression, but keep in mind that what a person thinks or believes is also a potential cause for depression. The following are the most common emotional symptoms and resultant mental states of those who are depressed.

> DEPRESSION IS MOST COMMONLY CHARACTERIZED BY THE BLUES— A DEEP SADNESS.

Sadness: *I feel awful!*
Depression is most commonly characterized by a deep sadness. The blues seem to creep up slowly and bring a spirit of heaviness. Crying and brooding are common for those who are in a funk. Some can hardly control the steady stream of tears. Depression is the antithesis of joy, which is a fruit of the Spirit: "A joyful heart makes a cheerful face, but when the heart is sad, the spirit is broken" (Prov. 15:13).

Despair: *It's hopeless!*
Despair is the absence of hope. Despair sees no light at the end of the tunnel, no hope at the end of the day and no answers for

the endless round of questions that plague the depressed mind. Three times the psalmist cried out, "Why are you in despair, O my soul? And why have you become disturbed within me? Hope in God, for I shall again praise Him for the help of His presence . . . for I shall yet praise Him, the help of my countenance and my God" (Ps. 42:5-11; see 43:5). Hope is the present assurance of some future good. The psalmist knew where his hope lay. Jeremy Taylor said, "It is impossible for a man to despair who remembers that his helper is omnipotent."[2] The problem is that depression seems to impede the normal process of memory.

Irritability and Low Frustration Tolerance: *I have had it with you!*
Depressed people have very little emotional reserve. Small things tick them off, and they are easily frustrated. They have low tolerance for the pressures of life. One lady said, "How can I plan for tomorrow when survival for the day is at the top of my list?"

Isolation and Withdrawal: *I'm going to my room!*
John Gray observed that men retreat to caves and women climb into holes.[3] Men tend to isolate more readily but spend less time in their caves than women do in holes. Most men are generally less image conscious and less introspective than women are. Many men will go away and lick their wounds and then come back as though nothing happened. It is hard for some men to reveal their souls. They tend to cover their pain with work or vices. Consequently, they are more likely to become workaholics or alcoholics.

People who suffer with depression pull away from others. They feel embarrassed to be with people when they feel so low. They don't want to be a wet blanket in the group and drag others down by their depression. Although some may think that isolation is a viable short-term solution, avoidance often adds to the downward spiral of depression.

Negative Thought Patterns: *Nothing is working; I'm such a failure!*
Generally speaking, depressed people have trouble thinking, concentrating and staying focused. Constant distractions rob them of mental peace. Just as water seeks the lowest ground, depression seeps into a person and drowns out optimism. It seems easier to see a problem, think the worst, predict failure, find fault and focus on weakness. First, depressed people have difficulty believing positive and good things about themselves. Feelings of worthlessness become the breeding ground for thoughts of self-destruction. They struggle with guilt that prompts them to become irrational, unreasonable and even delusional. Second, they cannot think positively about the future. They cannot stop worrying about tomorrow. It is not something they look forward to; it is something they dread. Third, the circumstances in which they find themselves are also interpreted as negative. This is the well-known depression triad that cognitive therapists see repeatedly in their patients.

Thoughts of Suicide: *Everybody would be better off if I were dead!*
Sadness, isolation, loss of energy, strained relationships and physical problems contaminate the depressed person's perspective of self and the future. Believing themselves to be helpless and hopeless, many depressed people begin to think of suicide as a way of escape.

In depressed states, people become self-absorbed. Mental exhaustion causes many to think negatively about themselves and less of others. They don't want to hear any more bad news or take on any more responsibility. It is a syndrome filled with misery, shame, sadness and guilt.

In Psalm 38, David expresses almost every symptom of depression listed above:

- somatic complaints (see v. 3)
- guilt and despair (see v. 4)
- irritability, low frustration tolerance, loss of appetite, sadness (see vv. 5-8)
- low energy and diminished activity (see v. 10)
- isolation and withdrawal (see v. 11)
- negative thoughts (see v. 12)
- thoughts of suicide (see v. 17)

David shares two keywords in this psalm that are necessary for recovery from a sense of helplessness and hopelessness: "For I *hope* in You, O LORD" (v. 15, emphasis added), and "Make haste to *help* me, O Lord, my salvation!" (v. 22, emphasis added).

DEPRESSION DIAGNOSIS

The following questionnaire can serve as an evaluation for depression and help determine whether the condition is mild or severe. Circle the number that would best describe you or the person you are concerned about. For instance, in response to the first item, circle 1 if you are exhausted all the time, 5 if you are a high-energy person or 3 if you have average energy, i.e., neither high nor low energy. Some mild depressions are a reaction to temporary setbacks or depressing circumstances that may last for a few hours or days. It is best to let such episodes pass, because they can momentarily skew the results. Wait a few hours or days in order to get a better reading of your general condition.

Evaluation

| 1. Low energy | 1 2 3 4 5 | High energy |
| 2. Difficulty sleeping or sleep all the time | 1 2 3 4 5 | Uninterrupted sleeping patterns |

3. No desire to be involved in activities	1	2	3	4	5	Very involved in activities
4. No desire for sex	1	2	3	4	5	Healthy sex drive
5. Aches and pains	1	2	3	4	5	Feel great
6. Loss of appetite	1	2	3	4	5	Enjoy eating
7. Sad (tearful)	1	2	3	4	5	Joyful
8. Despairing and hopeless	1	2	3	4	5	Hopeful and confident
9. Irritable (low frustration tolerance)	1	2	3	4	5	Pleasant (high frustration tolerance)
10. Withdrawn	1	2	3	4	5	Involved
11. Mental anguish	1	2	3	4	5	Peace of mind
12. Low sense of self-worth	1	2	3	4	5	High sense of self-worth
13. Pessimistic about the future	1	2	3	4	5	Optimistic about the future
14. Perceive most circumstances as negative and harmful to self	1	2	3	4	5	Perceive most circumstances as positive and as opportunities for growth
15. Self-destructive (I and others would be better off if I weren't here)	1	2	3	4	5	Self-preserving (I'm glad I'm here)

Interpretation
Add the numbers you circled to determine your total score   _____

continued on next page

If your total score is

45-75   You are likely not depressed.
35-44   You are mildly depressed.
25-34   You are depressed.
15-24   You are severely depressed.

Degrees of depression lie on a continuum from mild to severe. Everyone experiences mild depression due to the ups and downs of life. These mood fluctuations are generally related to health issues, mental attitudes and external pressures of living in a fallen world. In our experience, those who scored between 30 and 45 can manage their own recoveries and we hope that the contents of this book will help them do just that. Those who score lower than 30 should seek the help of a godly pastor, Christ-centered counselor or medical doctor if the cause is found to be endogenous (see chapter 2). They need the objectivity of someone else to help them resolve their conflicts.

INDICATOR LIGHTS

What are our emotions? Our emotions are to our soul what our ability to feel is to our body. Suppose I had the power to remove the sensation of pain and offered freedom from pain to you as a gift. Would you receive it? It sounds tempting, but if you could not feel pain, your body would be a mass of scars within weeks. The ability to feel pain is our protection from the harmful elements of the world. Depression is signaling that something is wrong.

Emotions are like the indicator lights on the control panels of our cars. There are three potential ways you can respond when the indicator light blinks on. You can ignore the warning by putting a piece of duct tape over it. That is called suppression and will prove to be unhealthy. It is also dishonest to cover up feelings in order to convince others that everything is okay.

Another option is to take a small hammer and break the light. That is called indiscriminate expression. It may be physically healthy for you to indiscriminately express your emotions, but it isn't for others. Be cautious about getting something off your chest or letting your feelings be known to all. In suppression, the hurting person pulls away. In indiscriminate expression, others pull away.

> OUR EMOTIONS ARE TO OUR
> SOUL WHAT OUR ABILITY TO
> FEEL IS TO OUR BODY.

The third option is to look under the hood to discover the cause; that is called acknowledgment. In others words, be honest about how you feel so that you can resolve the cause and live in harmony with God and others. In this book, we want to help you to look under the hood in order to discover the causes and cures of depression.

UNDERSTANDING BRAIN CHEMISTRY AND FINDING RELIEF

The endless cycle of idea and action,
Endless invention, endless experiment,
Brings knowledge of motion, but not of stillness;
Knowledge of speech, but not of silence;
Knowledge of words, and ignorance of the Word.
All our knowledge brings us nearer to our ignorance,
All our ignorance brings us nearer to death,
But nearness to death no nearer to GOD.

Where is the Life we have lost in living?
Where is the wisdom we have lost in knowledge?
Where is the knowledge we have lost in information?
The cycles of Heaven in twenty centuries,
Bring us farther from GOD and nearer to the Dust.

T. S. ELIOT

With the advancement of microcircuitry and the simplification of software, the depth of knowledge doubled every two-and-a-half years at the end of the twentieth century. If scientists and medical doctors now know far more about brain chemistry and how our neurological system functions than ever before, why has the number of people seeking treatment for depression nearly doubled in the last 10 years? Is there more than a neurological explanation for depression? Has our hope shifted from God to science? Has our thinking been either/or when it should be both/and?

Science and revelation are not on a collision course. God is the creator of all things, and He established the fixed order of the universe. Through the discipline of science, humankind has been able to study what God has created through empirical research. This is called general revelation. God intended that we interpret what we observe through the grid of special revelation, which is His Word. God's Word never changes, whereas a 50-year-old science book is not very accurate by today's standards. Who can predict what scientists will be saying 50 years from now about our present understanding of this world and its inhabitants?

Our hope in God is not incompatible with the natural sciences. Advances in research don't diminish the relevance of God, nor should they conflict with divine revelation. We are thankful for any advancement in medicine that will help alleviate human suffering.

WONDEROUS CREATION

God formed Adam from the dust of the earth and breathed life into him. This union of divine breath and earthly dust is what constitutes the makeup of every born-again child of God. We were designed to have an outer person and an inner person? (i.e., a material part and an immaterial part). The material, or physical, part of man relates to the external world through five senses. The inner person relates to God through the soul and spirit. Unlike the animal kingdom that operates by divine instinct, we have the capacity to think, feel and choose. Since we are "fearfully and wonderfully made" (Ps. 139:14), it only makes sense that God would create the outer person to correlate with the inner person, as diagram 2.1 illustrates.

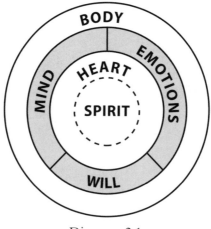

Diagram 2.1

The correlation between the mind and the brain is obvious, but there is a fundamental difference between the two. The brain is part of our physical body, but the mind is part of our soul, or inner person. In our present day, we have a wonderful analogy to illustrate the working relationship between the brain and the mind. Together they make up a very sophisticated computer system. Every computer operation is comprised of two distinct components: the hardware and the software. The hardware (the computer itself) is the brain in this analogy.

The brain functions much like a computer with its millions of switching transistors that code all the information in a binary numbering system of zeroes and ones. The miniaturization of circuitry has made it possible to store and compile an incredible amount of information in a computer the size of a notebook. However, humankind has not even come close to making a computer as sophisticated as the one that is now making it possible for you to read this book. A personal computer (PC) is mechanical, but our brains are living organisms composed of approximately 100 billion neurons. Each one is a living organism that in and of itself is a microcomputer. Every neuron is composed of a brain cell, an axon (stem) and many dendrites (inputs to the brain cell), as shown in diagram 2.2.

Neuron

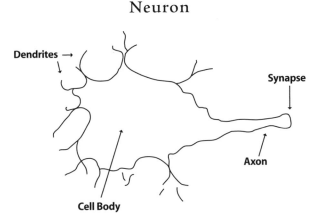

Diagram 2.2

Each brain cell has many inputs (dendrites) and only one output through the axon that channels neurotransmitters to other

dendrites. A myelin sheath covers the axon for insulation, because the cell sends electrochemical messages along the axon. Every neuron is connected to tens of thousands of other neurons. Given that there are 100 billion neurons, the potential number of combinations is mind boggling. There is a junction between the axon of one neuron and the dendrites of another called a synapse. Every brain cell receives information through its dendrites, which it processes, integrates and sends on to other neurons.

Neurotransmitters are produced in the axon. When a signal from the cell reaches the axon, it releases neurotransmitters that cross the synapse to other dendrites. There are approximately 40 different types of neurotransmitters—dopamine and serotonin are the most known and relevant to our discussion on depression. Only five percent of the serotonin is in the brain. The rest is traveling throughout the body's nervous system. This is basic anatomy, and we share it for the purpose of explaining possible causes and cures for endogenous depression.

BIPOLAR DEPRESSION

Depression is categorized as either bipolar or unipolar. A bipolar or manic-depressive illness has two poles: highs (manic moods) and lows (depressed moods). The manic symptoms include increased energy; unrealistic and grandiose beliefs in one's own power and ability; racing ideas and thoughts; poor judgment; increased talking or social activity; extreme euphoria; impulsivity; irritability and distractibility; obnoxious, insensitive or irritating behavior; and abuse of alcohol or drugs. Paranoid, delusional and psychotic thinking is also possible. Current estimates indicate that approximately one-half to one percent of the adult population suffers from manic depression, which means between 1 and 2 million Americans have had or will have this affliction.[1] Bipolar illness is equally common in men and women. It is typically a recurrent, or episodic, disorder. A 1973 study examined nearly 400 patients who had an episode of manic-depressive illness, and only two failed to have a recurrence.[2] One of the foremost experts of this illness, Kay Jamison, who struggled with manic depression herself, wrote a fascinating book that reveals the relationship between art or creativity and madness (mania).[3] Some of the most creative people in the world struggled with this illness: writers Hans Christian Anderson, John Bunyan, Samuel Clemens, Ralph Waldo Emerson, William Faulkner*, Ernest Hemingway*, Herman Melville, Robert Louis Stevenson, Tennessee Williams*, Virginia Woolf* and Leo Tolstoy; composers Irving Berlin*, Noel Coward, Stephen Foster, George Frederic Handel, Cole Porter, Robert Schumann* and Peter Tchaikovsky; and artists Michelangelo and Vincent van Gogh*.

Those individuals with an asterisk after their name spent time in an asylum or psychiatric hospital. Ernest Hemingway, Virginia Woolf and Vincent van Gogh committed suicide. In her autobiography *An Unquiet Mind*, Jamison describes her incredible accomplishments during her periods of mania.[4] Treating her illness with lithium brought her great relief, but it also decreased her creativity and productivity. She also said that taking medicine was not enough. She needed the objectivity of someone else to help her get through the depressive cycle. Like many who struggle with bipolar depression, her lows were so awful that suicide seemed the only way out. Leo Tolstoy shared what it was like during his low moments of depression:

The thought of suicide came to me as naturally then as the thought of improving life had come to me before. This thought was such a temptation that I had to use cunning against myself in order not to go through with it too hastily. I did not want to be in a hurry only because I wanted to use all my strength to untangle my thoughts.

If I could not get them untangled, I told myself, I could always go ahead with it. And there I was, a fortunate man, carrying a rope from my room, where I was alone every night as I undressed, so that I would not hang myself from the beam between the closets. And I quit going hunting with a gun, so that I would not be too easily tempted to rid myself of life. I myself did not know what I wanted. I was afraid of life. I struggled to get rid of it, and yet I hoped for something from it.

And this was happening to me at a time when, from all indications, I should have been considered a completely happy man; this was when I was not yet fifty years old. I had a good, loving, and beloved wife, fine children, and a large estate that was growing and expanding without any effort on my part. More than ever before I was respected by friends and acquaintances, praised by strangers, and I could claim a certain renown without really deluding myself.[5]

As in the case of Tolstoy, endogenous depressions may have little to do with external circumstances. This is a mental and physical struggle, or possibly a spiritual battle for the mind, as we will examine later. The transmission of a message through the brain cell requires a certain balance of sodium (positive) and chloride (negative) ions. Sodium chloride ($NaCl$) is a salt. In a similar fashion, electricity flows through copper better than it does through iron due to the chemical makeup of each substance.

In a bipolar illness, the balance and polarity of positive and negative ions is abnormal. In depression, the sodium ions increase about 50 percent, and with the mania they increase as much as 200 percent. The drug of choice for bipolar depression has been lithium carbonate, which is an inert salt. This reduces the number of sodium and chloride ions, which allows the transmission to proceed through the cell and into other neurons.

UNIPOLAR DEPRESSION

Unipolar depression affects nearly 10 percent of the American population and appears to be growing. Unipolar depression is a continuous low with no episodes of mania. Two major studies in the late 1970s revealed a *tenfold* increase in depression over the course of the last century![6] As noted earlier, the diagnosis of

> UNIPOLAR DEPRESSION AFFECTS NEARLY 10 PERCENT OF THE AMERICAN POPULATION AND APPEARS TO BE GROWING.

depression has nearly doubled since the mid-1980s. This tremendous increase in depression has experts everywhere proclaiming that the world is experiencing a blues epidemic.

The focus for *medically* curing unipolar depression has been on the production, preservation and transmission of neurotransmitters. Some of the earlier antidepressant drugs were monoamine oxidase inhibitors (MAOIs). The purpose of these medications was to block the action of monoamine oxidase, which is an enzyme that destroys certain neurotransmitters. Tricyclic antidepressants were the next generation of antidepressants. Their purpose was to keep the neurotransmitters in productive service longer. Presently more focus is on stimulating the production of mood-altering neurotransmitters, such as serotonin. The overall purpose of antidepressant medication is to get the brain functioning normally again so that the mind can think clearly and start the process of recovering physical energy, sex drive, sleep and the activities that make life meaningful.

Because of the advent of antidepressant medications in the mid 1950s, medical doctors now have a better understanding of brain chemistry and neurophysiology. However, it is incomplete to think of depression as purely a physical disorder requiring medication. Depression involves an inseparable combination of body, soul and spirit. If all three components are implicated in the initiation of depression, then all three areas should be avenues of intervention as well. Physical assessment and medical examinations are often warranted when depression is severe.

ANTIDEPRESSANT MEDICATIONS

There is a major difference between antidepressants and antipsychotic or antianxiety (tranquilizers) medications. The latter are sedatives (downers). They don't cure anything. They slow the mind down to inhibit distracting thoughts (or voices) or to allow the person to relax in order to get some rest from a mind that won't shut off. Antidepressant medications have the potential to cure some neurological conditions. Most of the modern antidepressants have fewer side effects and are not necessarily habit forming.

Serotonin is only one of many neurotransmitters in the brain, but it is the one most commonly linked to mood and has been the one most studied:

> Serotonin, or the lack of it, has been implicated not only in depression, uncontrollable appetite and obsessive-compulsive disorder but also in autism, bulimia, social phobias, premenstrual syndrome, anxiety and panic, migraines, schizophrenia and even extreme violence.[7]

Certain antidepressant medications enhance the availability of serotonin. Since there are no clinically available tests for serotonin, serotonin boosters are often used to help make a diagnosis. If the person's condition improves after taking boosters for four to six weeks, the doctor would conclude that they have a serotonin deficiency (i.e., a chemical imbalance). If no change is observed, the serotonin level is considered to be normal. These are not "happy pills," and they do not alter moods by themselves. They only work if they are needed and are relatively safe compared to most other drugs. Overdosing on pain relievers like acetaminophen and ibuprofen could be more dangerous than taking too much of a serotonin booster.

Even though medical doctors readily admit to a lack of precision with prescription drugs, these drugs are their primary means of treating depression. Serotonin-boosting medications currently make up 65 percent of a primary-care doctor's prescriptions for depression. Doctors have prescribed Prozac for approximately 20 million Americans. Over 600,000 children are currently on Prozac, which now comes in peppermint flavor. Choosing a serotonin medication that is right for you requires the assistance of your physician. There are a host of different antidepressant medications. If the first one doesn't bring the desired effect, a second one may be tried. There is no way your doctor can accurately measure your brain chemistry and production of neurotransmitters. The general procedure is to get a good reading of the symptoms and then prescribe a drug that has been helpful for others who had similar symptoms. A *Time* magazine article commented on the present level of understanding about serotonin:

> Despite years of study and impressive breakthroughs, researchers are only beginning to understand the chemical's complex role in the functioning of the body and

brain—and how doctors can make adjustments when serotonin levels go out of balance. So far, the tools used to manipulate serotonin in the human brain are more like pharmacological machetes than they are like scalpels—crudely effective but capable of doing plenty of collateral damage. Says Barry Jacobs, a neuroscientist at Princeton University: "We just don't know enough about how the brain works."[8]

Serotonin boosters are like a key that unlocks the gate regulating neurotransmitters in your brain. Since everyone has a different lock, you may need to try different keys until you find the one that fits. However, each key has only a 70 percent chance of working on the first try. The following is a brief description of the modern medications prescribed for depression:

1. Selective Serotonin Reuptake Inhibitors (SSRIs)
   SSRIs are popular and easy to use. Usually the dose you start on is the dose you stay on. They work well for all of the serotonin-deficiency conditions listed above. As a class, the SSRIs can cause sexual dysfunction and, in some cases, weight gain. Some studies show that SSRIs can cause disruption of sleep. Some physicians find it best to start this medication at half the normal dosage for the first week to allow the patient's body to adjust. Recent studies have revealed that these medications are not as selective as once thought. Stimulating one neurotransmitter may be accompanied by a decrease in others as the brain seeks to balance itself.

   a. Prozac
      Prozac has been around the longest of the antidepressants that target serotonin.

This drug tends to be more activating and usually works well with people who are lethargic. Prozac can cause sleep disturbances in some people.

b. Zoloft

In addition to increasing serotonin levels, this medication when taken in higher doses can also boost a neurotransmitter called dopamine. It is also used for people with attention deficit disorder. Zoloft can cause intestinal side effects in some people.

c. Paxil

This medication has a calming effect on most people and can be sedating to some. Paxil appears to work especially well on muscle conditions such as stress headaches, irritable bowel syndrome and fibromyalgia.

d. Luvox

Luvox has been used mostly for obsessive-compulsive disorder, but it can also be used for other serotonin-deficiency conditions. It may have more drug interactions than other SSRIs.

e. Lexapro

This is the latest SSRI. Present reports indicate that it may be the safest and cleanest, meaning fewer side effects.

2. Non-SSRI Antidepressants

a. Effexor

This medication can boost serotonin levels

at low doses, noradrenergic levels at medium doses and dopamine levels at high doses. This makes Effexor a good choice in the treatment of attention deficit disorder, muscle conditions and lethargic patients. Effexor has a lower incidence of sexual dysfunction than the SSRIs. Some people experience sleep disturbance on Effexor and, when this medication is discontinued, the patient must be weaned off gradually in order to avoid side effects.

b. Serzone

This medication boosts serotonin in a more natural way. Serzone has no dopamine effect and tends to be calming. This is a good choice when there is some anxiety present; it may work sooner than the others. This has been one of the few drugs that has been shown to normalize sleep. Serzone does not affect sex drive or weight. Like Effexor, this medication has to be started at low doses and increased slowly over a period of three to four weeks to allow the body to adapt.

c. Remeron

This is one of the most complete medications for depression. It stimulates the release of serotonin and norepinephrine. Sedation and weight gain are the main side effects.

d. Wellbutrin

This medication works by boosting dopamine levels and is useful for attention deficit disorder or addiction problems. Wellbutrin has been recently marketed for smoking cessation under the name Zyban. Like Serzone, this medication does not affect sex drive or weight. It can cause sleep disturbance in some people.

e. Ritalin

This medication is well known for its use in attention deficit disorder. It works by substituting for dopamine. Ritalin and similar drugs work very quickly, are considered mood altering and have a high habituation potential. This drug should be used only in specialized situations since there are so many other medications that are safer and, in most cases, more effective.

Ask your physician if there are medications that should be avoided when taking a serotonin booster. Alcohol should always be avoided when taking these or similar medications. If an antidepressant medication works for you, it is best to stay on it for a period of 9 to 12 months to achieve maximum benefit.[9] If you take a prescription medication, make sure you check with your doctor regularly. This is your responsibility, since doctors cannot check on all their patients. Keep these facts in mind: Each year the Food and Drug Administration (FDA) reviews about 25 new drugs for approval. For this task, the agency has a professional staff of over 1,500 doctors, scientists, toxicologists and statisticians. However, to monitor the safety of the more than 3,000 drugs already on the market and being prescribed to millions, the agency has a professional staff of just five doctors and one epidemiologist.[10] Because long-term monitoring is virtually nonexistent, David Kessler, past commissioner of the FDA, revealed that "only about 1% of serious events [side effects] are reported to the FDA."[11]

If you have been on an antidepressant for several months and sense you no longer need it, consult your doctor and be sure to slowly sequence off the medication. Those who go off too quickly may find symptoms of depression returning, indicating that they went off the meds too soon. Yet that might not be the case at all. They could be feeling symptoms of withdrawal from the medication, which only reinforces the belief that they need the medication, when in actuality they may not.

ELECTROCONVULSIVE THERAPY

Electroconvulsive therapy (ECT), or shock treatment as it is commonly called, is used to treat severe cases of endogenous depression in patients who do not respond to medication. It is one of the most misunderstood and questioned medical treatments for mental illness due primarily to perceived abuses in the past. ECT administers a small electrical shock to the brain that induces a convulsion. Muscle relaxants and a mild anesthetic are given to the patient so that the seizure is only slightly felt by the patient. Patients usually experience a mild amnesia with very little pain. One occasional side effect is short-term memory loss. Nobody knows why, but ECT seems to stimulate the production of neurotransmitters. In some cases, it is more effective than antidepressants and works faster with fewer side effects, but it isn't considered a long-term answer. Most physicians still see ECT as a last resort.

A WHOLISTIC SOLUTION

If you only read this far in the book, you may easily conclude that depression can be cured simply by taking the right medications. That would be unfortunate and inaccurate. Medications cannot change your circumstances or cause you to resolve personal and spiritual conflicts, but they may have the potential to jump-start the computer so that the proper program can run.

Psychologist Dr. David Antonuccio and his colleagues at the University of Nevada School of Medicine found in their research that "despite the conventional wisdom, the data suggests that there is no stronger medicine than psychotherapy in the treatment of depression, even if severe."[12] *Consumer Reports* recently reached similar conclusions. After 4,000 of its subscribers responded to the largest-ever survey on the use of therapy and/or drugs to treat depression, researchers at the Consumers Union determined that "psychotherapy alone worked as well as psychotherapy combined with medication, like Prozac and Xanax. Most people who took the drugs did feel they were helpful, but many reported side effects."[13] The reader should be cautioned, however, that such conclusions drawn from surveys filled out by the general population can easily be skewed and do not constitute valid research.

Such research brings up the critical question of causation. Which came first: external negative circumstances, poor mental evaluation of life, lack of faith in God or chemical imbalance? A depressed mood will likely accompany biochemistry changes in the body, but to say that changed biochemistry caused depression is as incomplete as saying a dead battery caused the car not to start. We must ask: What caused the battery to fail, and is there another reason that the car wouldn't start? Is the car out of gas? Was it a faulty alternator or a broken belt? Were the lights left on? Is the battery old and worn out? You can jump-start a car by using booster cables, which is enough if you just left the lights on. However, a good mechanic considers many other causes to ensure that the car continues to run well.

The fact that antidepressant medications help depressed people feel better is not even arguable. They do. On the other hand, taking medication every time you have a symptom of depression is like getting a jump-start every time your car won't start. The car is designed to function as a whole unit and so are we. After having been on an antidepressant medication for almost three weeks, a woman declared, "I didn't know the promises in the Bible were true for me until now." The proper use of medication enabled her to assume a responsible course of action.

Martin Seligman, a noted researcher on depression, reflected on the causes of depression:

> I have spent the last twenty years trying to learn what causes depression. Here is what I think. Bipolar depression (manic-depression) is an illness of the body, biological in origin and containable by drugs. Some unipolar depressions, too, are partly biological, particularly the fiercest ones. Some unipolar depression is inherited. If one of two identical twins is depressed, the other is somewhat more likely to be depressed than if they'd been fraternal twins. This kind of unipolar depression can often be contained with drugs, although not nearly as successfully as bipolar depression can be, and its symptoms can often be relieved by electroconvulsive therapy.
>
> Since inherited unipolar depressions are in the minority, it raises the question of where the great number of depressions making up the epidemic in this country come from. I ask myself if human beings have undergone physical changes over the century that have made them more vulnerable to depression. Probably not. It is very doubtful that our brain chemistry or our genes have changed radically over the last two generations. Therefore, a tenfold increase in depression is not

likely to be explained on biological grounds.

I suspect that the epidemic depression so familiar to all of us is best viewed as psychological. My guess is that most depression starts with problems in living and with specific ways of thinking about these problems.[14]

We generally agree with Seligman, but we disagree that all severe unipolar and bipolar depression is only a physical illness of the body. It certainly can be the problem, and physical and chemical imbalances should definitely be considered in severe cases. However, we have found that many severe depressions have a definite spiritual component, which is overlooked in the secular world and often in our churches. (We will discuss that possibility in following chapters.) To illustrate this point, read the following testimony:

> I am writing in regards to your seminar in Minnesota. The day it was to start, I was to be admitted to a hospital for the fifth time for manic depression. I have been dealing with this for almost two years. We had gone to several doctors and tried about every drug they could think of. I also had shock treatments. I attempted suicide twice. Unable to work any longer, I spent most of my days downstairs wishing I were dead or planning my next attempt. Also, it was a good place to protect myself from people and the world around me. I had a history of self-abuse. I have spent 30-odd years in jail or prisons. I was a drug addict and an alcoholic. I have been in drug and alcohol treatment 28 times.
>
> I became a Christian several years ago but always lived a defeated life. Now I was going back to the hospital to try new medications or more shock treatments. My wife and friends convinced me your seminar would be of more

value. The hospital was concerned because they believed
I needed medical help. As the four days of the conference
progressed my head started to clear up! The Word of God
was ministering to me, even though I was confused and in
pain. I told one of your staff that I was in my eleventh
hour. He set up an appointment for me.

The session lasted seven hours. They didn't leave one
stone uncovered. The session was going great until
I came to bitterness and unforgiveness. The three things
that motivated my life were low self-esteem, anger and
bitterness, which were the result of being molested by a
priest and suffering from many years of physical and ver-
bal abuse in my childhood. I can honestly say I forgave
them and God moved right in, lifting my depression. My
eyes were now open to God's truth. I felt lighter than
ever before.

I did go to the hospital, but after two days they said
I didn't need to be there. My doctors said I was a differ-
ent person. They had never seen a person change so fast.
They said, "Whatever you are doing, don't stop." I have
been growing in the Lord daily. There is so much before
Christ and after Christ that I could go on forever.

Secular counselors seldom if ever see that kind of resolution.
Too many people continue in their depression because they have
considered only one possible cause and therefore only one possible cure. One Christian said, "My problem is neurological and
my psychiatrist says I shouldn't let anyone tell me differently."
She did admit that she hadn't found the right combination of
drugs yet, but she had all the hope in the world that she eventually would. Even though she was still depressed, her hope was in
finding the right combination of medications. In the same
church, another Christian said, "Taking medication demon-

strates a lack of faith." Of course he had never experienced depression! How could two people in the same church draw such diverse opinions?

God relates to us as whole people—body, soul and spirit—who live in a physical *and* spiritual world. Consider again our computer analogy: The brain represents the hardware and the mind represents the software. The tendency of the Western world is to assume that mental and/or emotional problems are primarily caused by faulty hardware. There is no question that organic brain syndrome, Alzheimer's disease or chemical or hormonal imbalances can impede our ability to function. The best program won't work if the computer is turned off or is in disrepair.

Therefore, it is a tragedy for a godly pastor or Christ-centered counselor to try helping a person who is physically sick without suggesting some medical attention. On the other hand, for medical doctors to think that they can cure the whole person with medication is equally tragic. Taking a pill to cure the body is commendable, but taking a pill to cure the soul is deplorable. Fortunately, most doctors know that the medical model can take you only so far. Many in the medical profession acknowledge that a majority of their patients are suffering for emotional and spiritual reasons (i.e., psychosomatic illnesses).

In dealing with mental or emotional disorders, we don't believe the primary problem is the hardware. We believe it is the software. Other than submitting our body to God as a living sacrifice and being good stewards of our physical body, we can't do a whole lot to change the hardware, but we can totally change the software. How we think and what we choose to believe can actually change our biochemistry.

MIND GAMES

And by a strange alchemy of brain His pleasure always turned to pain,
His naiveté to wild desire, His wit to love—His wine to fire and so, being
young and dipt in folly I fell in love with melancholy.

EDGAR ALLAN POE

Jim walked into my office physically shaking and totally defeated. For the past six months he had been hospitalized in a veterans administration (VA) hospital for severe depression. He was nearing retirement from a good civil service job, and the government was generously holding his position open for his return. The government's willingness to do so would soon come to an end, however, and the knowledge of that only contributed to his depression.

Jim would have good retirement benefits if he completed his career in the next two years, and his present financial status was well above average. Six months earlier he had made a substantial financial investment in a housing project that busted. At the time he wasn't sure if he would lose his investment, but there was little doubt in his own mind that hearing the bad news is what precipitated his depression. I asked him if he could recall any dominant thoughts that he was thinking at that time. He said, "I was sitting alone in my study considering what to do when the thought came to me, *You're going down*." And he believed it! But it wasn't true. His financial picture was far better than most.

I asked him if he would like to resolve these issues, and he agreed to go through *The Steps to Freedom in Christ* (the Steps).[1] We dealt with many issues and renounced the lie that he was "going down." Three hours later he was sitting calmly before me with peace of mind and a sense of hope for the first time in months. How does one explain such an abrupt change, and can it last? To do this, we need to understand how the body (material, or outer, self), soul and spirit (immaterial, or inner, self) function together with the external world and our creator.

HOW OUR COMPUTER GOT PROGRAMMED

Before we came to Christ, we were spiritually dead in our trespasses and sins (see Eph. 2:1). In other words, we were born physically alive but spiritually dead. We had neither the presence of God in our lives nor the knowledge of His ways. Consequently, we all learned to live our lives independently of God. From the earliest days our mind was programmed by the external world. That is why the heart of an unregenerate person is deceitful and desperately sick (see Jer. 17:9). Our worldview and attitudes about life were shaped by the environment in which we were raised in two different ways: (1) through prevailing experiences, such as the home in which we were raised, the neighborhood in which we played, the friends we had, and the church to which we did or didn't go; and (2) through traumatic experiences, such as the death of a family member, the divorce of parents, and emotional, sexual or physical abuse. These lasting impressions were burned into our mind over time through repetition or by the intensity of powerful experiences, both good and bad.

We live our lives according to what we have chosen to believe about ourselves and the world around us. We aren't always aware that we are continuously gathering information that forms, alters or intensifies our beliefs. Many cruise through life with a carefree attitude, unaware of how they are being influenced by the world in which they live. The external sources of information vary greatly from one culture to another. There is no value-neutral culture. We all have some safe and healthy input from our surroundings, as well as contaminated and unhealthy external stimuli, which affects our worldviews and perceptions of ourselves. Our belief system is always changing as we process positive and negative information and experiences. Unfortunately, not every piece of information we receive comes clearly marked as productive or unproductive, good or evil, true or false!

HOW OUR MIND IS REPROGRAMMED

Without the gospel, we all would be nothing more than products of our pasts. Ezekiel prophesied that God would put a new heart and a new spirit within us (see Ezek. 36:26), which actually happened when we were born again. We became a new creation in Christ (see 2 Cor. 5:17), and we now have the mind of Christ (see 1 Cor. 2:16) in the very center of our being. Then why don't we think differently and feel better? Because everything that has been previously programmed into our computers from the external world is still there and subject to recall. Nobody pushed the clear button, because there isn't one. Our mental computer has no delete button, therefore, it needs to be reprogrammed. The lies of this world must be replaced by the truth of God's Word:

> And do not be conformed to this world, but be transformed by the renewing of your mind, so that you may prove what the will of God is, that which is good and acceptable and perfect (Rom. 12:2).

Before we came to Christ, we were conformed to this world, and we will continue to be if we allow ourselves to be influenced by it. Messages from this world are still being received by our brain and interpreted by our mind, but now we have a totally

> BEFORE WE CAME TO CHRIST, WE WERE CONFORMED TO THIS WORLD, AND WE WILL CONTINUE TO BE IF WE ALLOW OURSELVES TO BE INFLUENCED BY IT.

new internal input, "which is Christ in you, the hope of glory" (Col. 1:27). The Spirit of truth will lead us into all truth, and that truth will set us free (see John 8:32).

HOW THE OUTER SELF AND INNER SELF CORRELATE

Let's see how the rest of the outer self correlates with the inner self. The brain and the spinal cord make up the central nervous system, which splits off into a peripheral nervous system (see diagram 3.1). The peripheral nervous system has two channels: the autonomic nervous system and the somatic nervous system. The somatic nervous system regulates our muscular and skeletal movements, such as speech and gestures or any body movement over which we have volitional control. It obviously correlates to our will. We don't do anything without first thinking it. The thought-action response is so rapid that we are hardly aware of the sequence, but it is always there. Involuntary muscular movements can occur when the system breaks down, as is the case with Parkinson's disease (shaking palsy), which is a progressive degeneration of nerve cells in one part of the brain that controls muscle movements.

Diagram 3.1

Our autonomic nervous system regulates our internal organs. We do not have direct volitional control over our glands. They function automatically. In a general sense, we don't have volitional control over our emotions either. We cannot will ourselves to feel good or to like somebody. We do, however, have control of what we think, and we can decide to believe that what God says is true. Just as our glands are regulated by our central nervous system, our emotions are primarily a product of our thoughts. It is not the circumstances of life that determine how we feel; instead, it is primarily determined by how we interpret life events (i.e., what we choose to think and believe) and, secondarily, by how we choose to behave. Between the external stimulus and the emotional response is the brain (receiver) and the mind (interpreter). Negative external circumstances do not cause depression. We can, however, become depressed by interpreting circumstances with something less than a biblical worldview.

How Stress Becomes Distress

Let's apply this to the problem of stress. When external pressures put demands on our physical system, our adrenal glands respond by secreting cortisone-like hormones into our physical body. Our body automatically respond to external pressures. This is the natural fight-or-flight response to the pressures of life. If the pressures persist too long, our adrenal glands can't keep up, and stress becomes distress. The result can be physical illness, or we may become irritated with things that wouldn't bother us physically or emotionally in less stressful times.

Why do two people respond differently to the same stressful situation? Some actually seize the opportunity and thrive under the pressure while others fall apart. What is the difference between the two? Does one have superior adrenal glands? Although we may differ considerably in physical condition, the major difference lies in the mind. It isn't just the external factors that determine the degree of stress. We all face the pressures of deadlines, schedules, traumas and temptations. The major difference is how we mentally interpret the external world and process the data our brains receive.

Our mind can choose to respond by trusting God with the assurance of victory or by seeing ourselves as helpless victims of circumstance. The Israelites saw Goliath in reference to themselves and stressed out, while David saw Goliath in reference to God and triumphed. Faith in God (i.e., what we believe) greatly affects how we interpret and respond to the world's pressures.

> OUR MIND CAN CHOOSE TO RESPOND BY TRUSTING GOD WITH THE ASSURANCE OF VICTORY OR SEEING OURSELVES AS THE HELPLESS VICTIMS OF CIRCUMSTANCE.

It is important to understand that the adrenal glands do not initiate the release of adrenaline. They are the responders, not the initiators. Hormones are released into the bloodstream after the brain records the external inputs and the mind interprets them. The brain itself can only function according to how it has been programmed. God created us with some natural programming for survival, such as a newborn baby's sucking instinct and other necessary bodily functions that sustain life. These natural behaviors are similar to how the animal kingdom functions through divine instincts.

There is also a natural, or normal, production of neurotransmitters that allows the brain to function; otherwise, no physical life could be sustained in infancy. In other words, we are programmed from birth to physically exist. We have a natural will to live and seek food, clothing, shelter and safety. Could the programming of our mind or how we choose to think affect how the brain operates? If the secretion of adrenaline from our adrenal glands is triggered by how we think or perceive reality, could serotonin or other neurotransmitters be affected by how we think and choose to believe?

Does the presence of God in our lives transform the outer self or the inner self? What physically changed in our lives at the moment we were born again? In a similar fashion, what physical changes might you observe in your computer when you slip in a new program? Even though the same number of hardware components exist in the computer, the screen shows a different output. The electronic flow through the computer changed. Would we begin to live differently if a new program was loaded into our brain? Yes, because our eyes would be opened to the truth, and the presence of the Holy Spirit enables us to live by faith. The flow of neurotransmitters would certainly change even though the number of brain cells would remain the same.

Indeed, the presence of God in our lives affects even our physical being. According to Paul, "He who raised Christ Jesus from the dead will also give life to your mortal bodies through His Spirit who dwells in you" (Rom. 8:11). This is evident when we walk by the Spirit, since "the fruit of the Spirit is love [the character of God], joy [the antithesis of depression], peace [the antithesis of anxiety], patience [the antithesis of anger], kindness, goodness, faithfulness, gentleness, self-control; against such things there is no law" (Gal. 5:22-23). The connection between the initiating cause (the Spirit of truth) and the end result (self-control) is the mind, which directs the brain and in turn regulates all our glands and muscular movements.

HOW BIBLICAL FAITH
DEVELOPS WHOLENESS

Jesus asked the blind men, "'Do you believe that I am able to do this?' They said to Him, 'Yes, Lord.' Then He touched their eyes, saying, 'It shall be done to you according to your faith'" (Matt. 9:28-29). The blind men chose to believe; therefore, the external power of Jesus was made effective. In other words, the Lord chose to bring about a physical healing through the channel of their belief. Is this not true in every aspect of life? We are saved by faith (see Eph. 2:8) and sanctified by faith (see Gal. 3:3-5), and we walk, or live, by faith (see 2 Cor. 5:7). God never bypasses our mind. He works through it, and we are transformed by the renewing of our mind. He makes possible the renewing of our mind by His very presence in our lives. We respond in faith by choosing to believe the truth and live by the power of the Holy Spirit, and not carrying out the desires of the flesh (see Gal. 5:16). Jesus is "the way [how we ought to live], and the truth [what we ought to believe], and the life [our spiritual union with God]" (John 14:6). Even the operation of spiritual gifts incorporates the use of our mind. Paul concludes, "I will pray with the spirit and I will pray with the mind also; I will sing with the spirit and I will sing with the mind also" (1 Cor. 14:15).

HOW GOD'S TRUTH BRINGS FREEDOM

If truth sets us free and faith transforms our lives, then how is our neurological system affected? Scientific studies shed light on the relationship between learned helplessness and neurochemical changes in the body. Demitri and Janice Papolos describe an experiment where rats were "taught" helplessness by the use of shock. The doctors were able to measure neurological changes at various beta receptor sites indicating depression:

> Dr. Henn and his colleagues induced depression in another group of rats, but treated them without medication. They made a behavioral intervention and "taught" the rats how to escape the shock. Actually, a

medical student working in the lab knit the rats little sweaters with long sleeves over their front paws. Strings were attached to the sleeves and the researchers could pull the rat's paws up, marionette-like, and train them to push the lever that would stop the shock. With the rats no longer helpless, their symptoms of depression abated, and the beta receptor sites returned to their previous state. Dr. Henn and others have concluded from these studies that, just as neurochemistry affects behavior, changes in behavior affect neurochemistry.

Complementary findings have been found in the treatment of human depression. A brief psychotherapeutic treatment called cognitive therapy focuses on the thought processes of a depressed person, in particular the hopeless and helpless thinking, and by changing the negative thought patterns, has proved to be as effective as the antidepressant imipramine in treating the depression.[2]

Research reveals the link between brain chemistry and hope. Our body is affected if we think we are helpless, hopeless and out of control. Symptoms of depression such as sadness, despair, lethargy, loss of appetite and sleep problems increase. Once hope is restored, depression leaves. This has tremendous implications for those who struggle with depression and those who minister to them. God established faith as the means by which we relate to Him and live our lives. Since He doesn't bypass our mind, then neither should we.

If the way we perceive reality and choose to believe affects our physiology and biochemistry, then treatment for depression should not be limited to medications. If that is the case, should a Christian ever take medications for emotional problems? Perhaps an analogy is the best way to answer that question. Suppose you were suffering regularly from acid indigestion because of your eating habits. Should you take medication to relieve the heartburn? Most people would, and there is nothing wrong with getting temporary relief, but the long-term answer is to change your eating habits. Your body is telling you something: Stop feeding me this junk! Your body is a product of what you eat, drink and breathe. There is also the possibility that you have a serious stomach illness such as an ulcer or cancer. Such symptoms could also indicate a heart problem.

Taking medication to relieve pain is advisable, but a wise person will seek to know the original cause of the condition. A lifestyle change may be necessary if the person wants to live a healthy life. Good health is a product of a balanced routine of rest, exercise and a healthy diet. No matter how well we learn to take care of our physical body, it is still destined to deteriorate over the course of our natural lives. Yet our hope doesn't lie in preservation of our mortal body; our hope lies in proven character (see Rom. 5:4) and the final resurrection when we will receive our resurrected, immortal body. "Therefore we do not lose heart, but though our outer man is decaying, yet our inner man is being renewed day by day" (2 Cor. 4:16).

If negative thinking affects neurochemistry, then taking antidepressants may be advisable to alleviate the depressed mood, but it is not the long-term solution in the majority of cases. The danger is to establish our reliance on medication for the cure of depression instead of establishing our hope in God and learning to live a balanced life according to what He says is true. However, we must also be open to the possibility that there may be an organic brain problem such as encephalitis, another viral infection or a chemical imbalance that comes from a decaying body living in a fallen world.

There is also the possibility that some people will have to live with the physical consequences of depression for long periods of time. It may do lasting damage to their neurological systems.

Certain medications may be necessary for the rest of their lives. It is similar to alcoholics who have done irreparable damage to their livers. The Lord may heal such a person in response to prayer, but Scripture gives no absolute assurance of that happening. There would be little incentive for us not to sin or believe incorrectly if the natural consequences were removed.

We have been programmed by our Western culture to search for every natural explanation first. If no explanation is found, then there is nothing left to do but pray. However, the Bible reads differently. In the context of explaining how faith in God is the answer for anxiety, Jesus concludes:

> But seek first His kingdom and His righteousness, and all these things will be added to you. So do not worry about tomorrow; for tomorrow will care for itself (Matt. 6:33-34).

When we struggle with emotional problems, go to God *first*, as He instructs us to do!

HOW OUR THOUGHTS AND BELIEFS ARE CHANGED

In chapter 2 we learned that physical pain is necessary for our self-preservation. Similarly, the presence of emotional pain stimulates the process of renewing our mind and the development of our character. Let's look at the inner human to gain a better understanding of how our thinking affects our emotions. Even though we have very little direct control over our emotions, we can change how we think and what we believe. Many secular cognitive therapists such as Albert Ellis and Aaron Beck teach that our emotions are essentially a product of our thoughts. They believe that the primary source of depression is the way people perceive themselves, their circumstances and their futures, which is referred to as the depression triad. Several Christian counselors such as William Backus and David Stoop say essentially the same thing.[3]

Cognitive (mental) therapy is based on the premise that people do what they do and feel what they feel because of what they choose to think and believe. Therefore, if we want to change how we behave or feel, we should change what we think and believe. From a Christian perspective, that is repentance. If we possess distorted, false or negative beliefs about God, ourselves and the world, then we disagree with what God says about Himself, us and the world we live in. This "disagreement" is missing the mark; it is sin. "Whatever is not from faith is sin" (Rom. 14:23). Christians repent when they agree with God that what they believe is not true and what they do is not right, and then they turn from those lies and false beliefs. Confession is agreeing with God. Repentance happens when old, worldly beliefs are substituted with Christian beliefs based on God's Word. The word "repentance" in the original Greek language literally means, "a change of mind," which must happen if we are going to live a liberated life in Christ.

HOW IMPORTANT TRUTH IS

Returning to the story at the beginning of this chapter, Jim was depressed because he believed a lie about himself and his financial condition. He chose to believe that he was "going down," even though that wasn't true. The failed financial investment and the possible loss of money did not cause the depression. Rather, his interpretation of the facts and the lies he believed about himself caused the depression.

As I sat and listened to Jim's story, it didn't make sense to me why he was feeling depressed because of his financial situation, which at the time was far better off than mine. I thought at the time, *You are far better off financially than I am, so there is no good reason for you to be depressed.* Telling people they shouldn't feel a certain way not only is less than helpful, but it is also condemning. It is better and more accurate to suggest that they may not be interpreting the data correctly or seeing the situation from the right perspective. If what a person believes does not conform to truth, then what he or she feels does not conform to reality. The vast majority of people around the world had far more reason to be depressed about their finances than Jim did, but he couldn't change how he felt—none of us can. To make matters worse, the VA hospital staff had medicated him to the point of numbness, but they never made the connection between his thoughts and his feelings.

Suppose you have been employed most of your adult life by a major company that is downsizing. On Monday you receive a message from your boss saying that he wants to see you Friday at 10:30 A.M. Why does he want to see you Friday morning? Is he going to lay you off? If you think he is, you may initially get angry. When you start thinking that maybe he is and then again maybe he isn't, you are double-minded and therefore anxious. By Wednesday you are sure you are going to be laid off and start to feel depressed when you think of how hopeless your situation may be: *Where am I going to get a job at my age? How are we going to afford college for our kids?* By Friday you are an emotional basket case. When you enter his office, he says, "Congratulations, we are making you a vice president," and you faint on the spot! All the emotions you felt that week did not conform to reality, because what you believed did not reflect truth.

HOW EVERY THOUGHT IS
TAKEN CAPTIVE

The most damaging thoughts that we entertain are lies about ourselves and God (see chapter 4). The apostle Paul makes a critical connection in 2 Corinthians between thoughts that we have toward God and the potential spiritual battle going on for our mind:

> For though we live in the world, we do not wage war as the world does. The weapons we fight with are not the weapons of the world. On the contrary, they have divine power to demolish strongholds. We demolish arguments and every pretension that sets itself up against the knowledge of God, and we take captive every thought to make it obedient to Christ (10:3-5, *NIV*).

Computer programmers coined the acronym, "GIGO," which means garbage in, garbage out. If we put garbage into our mind, we will live a pretty smelly life. Jesus said, "The good man out of the good treasure of his heart brings forth what is good; and the evil man out of the evil treasure brings forth what is evil; for his mouth speaks from that which fills his heart" (Luke 6:45). We must be very careful what we put into our mind. It doesn't make any difference whether our thoughts originate from the TV, the radio, a book, a speaker, from our own memory banks, from the pit or whether they are original thoughts of our own. We must take every thought captive to the obedience of Christ.

If what you think is not true according to God's Word, then you do not pay attention to your thoughts. Instead, you do what the apostle Paul says, "Finally, brethren, whatever is true, whatever is honorable, whatever is right, whatever is pure, whatever is lovely, whatever is of good repute, if there is any excellence and if anything worthy of praise, dwell on these things" (Phil. 4:8). You don't get rid of negative thoughts by trying not to think them, you overcome them by choosing the truth until the truth drowns out and completely replaces the negative thoughts. If you want to experience the freedom that Christ purchased for you and the peace of mind that surpasses all understanding (see Phil. 4:7), then choose to think only those thoughts that perfectly align with the Word of God.

HOW VIRUSES ARE DETECTED

Computer owners have been warned about the potential for their computer to contract a virus. A virus can go undetected and cause severe damage to programs already loaded in the computer. Likewise, it is not always easy to detect a virus in our own belief systems, because the major strategy of the enemy is deception. As believers, we should not pay attention to tempting, accusing and deceiving thoughts. We are to put on the armor of God, take up the shield of faith and stand against Satan's fiery darts aimed at our mind.

The most devious of Satan's schemes is deception, because if we are tempted we know it and if we are accused we know it, but if we are deceived we don't know it. From the very beginning, Satan was deceiving us. In the Garden of Eden, Eve was deceived by Satan and believed a lie. That is why Jesus prays for those who follow Him, "I do not ask You to take them out of the world, but to keep them from the evil one. Sanctify them in the truth; Your word is truth" (John 17:15,17). Paul wrote, "But I am afraid that, as the serpent deceived Eve by his craftiness, your minds will be led astray from the simplicity and purity of devotion to Christ" (2 Cor. 11:3). Commenting on the later days of the Church age, Paul writes, "But the Spirit explicitly says that in later times some will fall away from the faith, paying attention to deceitful spirits and doctrines of demons" (1 Tim. 4:1).

We have seen evidence of this all over the world. People struggle with their thoughts, have difficulty concentrating and hear "voices." These "voices," or negative thoughts, are usually self-condemning, suicidal, delusional, blasphemous and phobic, which result in feelings of guilt, hopelessness, sadness and deep despair. These symptoms are what therapists typically associate with severely depressed people—both bipolar and unipolar. If anybody thought those kinds of thoughts, of course he or she would be depressed. If a depressed person shared those symptoms with a secular therapist or a doctor, the therapist or doctor would assume that a chemical imbalance was the cause and would likely place the client on some kind of antipsychotic medication and/or antidepressant.

We have to be careful not to rule out the need for medications, but serious questions need to be asked. How can a chemical produce a personality or a thought, and how can our neurotransmitters randomly fire in such a way as to produce a thought that we are opposed to thinking? That concept is hard to believe. It should be much easier for Christians to believe that those negative thoughts are patterns of the flesh learned from living in a fallen world or fiery darts from Satan, which Scripture clearly warns us about. A therapist with a secular worldview would not even consider such a possibility.

Condemning, blasphemous and deceiving thoughts often reveal a battle for the mind. In such cases, we help people resolve their personal and spiritual conflicts by submitting to God and resisting the devil (see Jas. 4:7). The intervention we use is *The Steps to Freedom in Christ*. Potentially every born-again Christian should be able to experience "the peace of God, which surpasses all understanding, will guard your hearts and minds through Christ Jesus" (Phil. 4:7, *NKJV*). Most Christians, however, are not experiencing their freedom in Christ, but they could. God desires it for all His children.

At the end of a Living Free in Christ conference (a conference of Freedom in Christ Ministries), attendees were given an opportunity to go through the Steps. About 85 percent can process the Steps in the final group session. The rest are offered an appointment for a private session with a well-trained encourager. A pretest was given and then a posttest three months later, which showed the following results in percentage of improvement:

Diagram 3.2

	Oklahoma City, OK	Tyler, TX
Depression	44%	57%
Anxiety	45	54
Fear	48	49
Anger	36	55
Tormenting thoughts	51	50
Negative habits	48	53
Sense of self-worth	52	56

Jesus is the wonderful counselor. Only He can grant repentance leading to a knowledge of the truth (see 2 Tim. 2:25), bind up the brokenhearted and set the captive free. It is important to keep in mind that the Steps don't set you free. Who sets you free is Christ, and what sets you free is your response to Him in repentance and faith. This process of helping people repent is certainly not new but is often overlooked in helping people who struggle, which is probably one reason why our society is experiencing a blues epidemic. We cannot experience the fruit of the Spirit if we are believing a lie, dabbling in the occult, holding on to our bitterness, sinking in pride, living in rebellion or sinning. The depressed mind is riddled with deceptive thoughts and erroneous beliefs built upon contradictions and lies. Those issues must be resolved in order to experience the peace of God, which guards our heart and our mind. To illustrate, read the following testimony a friend of our ministry shared:

A year ago, Simon fell captive to severe depression. The doctors did what they could, but without much effect. From time to time I had the opportunity to speak with him about the love of Christ, but he wasn't very responsive. Last fall we began to meet more frequently, but I always came away frustrated. Nothing seemed to change, and our conversations ran in circles around the same morbid themes. However, God used these times to show me that I was relying too much on my own efforts and not nearly enough on His power to effect change. In desperation, I was driven to seek God in a more profound way through prayer. God worked on Simon's distorted view of truth, while he worked to cut through the pride that was in my own heart. Just before Christmas, Simon made a commitment to follow Christ as Lord and Savior. His depression, however, only mildly improved.

Simon had a history of occult and new age involvement, and it became evident that there was demonic oppression in his life. For this reason, I loaned him *The Bondage Breaker*. At the end of the book the believer is invited to walk through the seven Steps to freedom in Christ. I told Simon that I would help him work through the Steps when I returned from a trip. During our time away, I called Simon to see how he was doing. The voice that spoke to me was changed. Simon had not waited for me to take him through the Steps. He had done it himself the previous evening. The old thoughts which had constantly filled his mind were gone. I heard him laughing for the first time. Praise the Lord.

CHAPTER FOUR

THE BASIS
FOR HOPE

Dearest,
I feel certain I am going mad again. I feel we can't go through
another of those terrible times. And I shan't recover this time. I begin to hear
voices, and I can't concentrate. So I am doing what seems the best thing to do.
You have given me the greatest possible happiness. You have been in every
way all that anyone could be. I don't think two people could have been
happier till this terrible disease came. I can't fight any longer.

VIRGINIA WOOLF, A FINAL LETTER TO HER HUSBAND

The above quote is the first lines in the recent movie *The Hours*.[1] It depicts the life and tragic death of author Virginia Woolf and two other related stories. The connection between the three stories is revealed in the movie. Each of the three stories centers around female characters who struggle with depression, one of whom commits suicide. Another character who also kills himself, played by Ed Harris, refers to the never-ending agony as "hours." Hours and hours of torment that never seem to end. One can't help but wonder if Virginia Woolf was paying attention to a deceiving spirit. Based on our experience of counseling hundreds of people, we believe she probably was. How tragic, because it is so resolvable.

Depression is a sense of hopelessness. If I wanted to take away your hope, all I would have to do is distort your concept of God and your understanding of who you are as a child of God. Ask people who have been depressed for any length of time what their concept of God is and what they believe about themselves. You will hear people questioning God and salvation, or believing things about themselves and God that are not true. Visit a psychiatric ward in a hospital and you will find very religious people, but what they believe about themselves and God is usually totally distorted. To illustrate this point, read Psalm 13:

> How long, O LORD? Will You forget me forever? How long will You hide Your face from me? How long shall I take counsel in my soul, having sorrow in my heart all the day? How long will my enemy be exalted over me? Consider and answer me, O LORD my God; enlighten my eyes, or I will sleep the sleep of death, and my enemy will say, "I have overcome him," and my adversaries will rejoice when I am shaken. But I have trusted in Your lovingkindness; my heart shall rejoice in Your salvation. I will sing to the LORD, because He has dealt bountifully with me.

David shares classic symptoms of depression including hopelessness, negative self-talk, sadness and thoughts of death. Even though he believes in God, David is depressed because what he believes about God is not true. How can an omnipresent and omniscient God forget David for even one minute much less forever? Taking "counsel in my soul" is nothing more than self-talk or mental rumination, which is unproductive. Finally, David asks God to enlighten his eyes, and by the end of Psalm 13, his reason has returned. David remembers that he trusts in God's loving-kindness. Then he expresses hope that his heart shall again rejoice, and he exercises his will by singing to the Lord.

DISLODGE DISTORTED CONCEPTS

Like every other perception of reality, much of what we believe about God was formed by the environment in which we were raised. If we were fortunate enough to have been raised in a loving Christian home where the Word of God was honored, then our perceptions of God could be fairly accurate. Although, some legalistic churches and homes that know little of God's grace can produce children who have a very distorted concept of their heavenly Father.

Consider the depressed pastor's wife who came to see me. I asked, "You really love Jesus, don't you?" She affirmed that she did. Then I asked, "You really love the Holy Spirit, don't you?" Again she agreed. "But you don't like your heavenly Father, do you?" She began to cry. She had a very abusive mother, but that wasn't her primary struggle. Her father was the problem. He sat like a lump and let her be abused. In her distorted thinking, that is what her heavenly Father does.

I gave her a set of audiocassettes by A. W. Tozer on the attributes of God. She listened to them three times, but the impact was nil. Just telling people like her the truth about God and who they are in Christ is often not enough. The nature of God will never change, but our perception of Him has been filtered through the grid of living in a fallen world (see diagram 4.1). I have seen good students of the Bible point to the left side of the diagram when asked, "Which side reveals the true nature of God?" When asked how they feel about God in their personal experience, they may point to the right side! Sometime in their experience of growing up, they entertained untrue thoughts about God. If what we believe does not conform to truth, then what we feel does not conform to reality. Consequently, there are people in our churches who intellectually know that God loves them, but they don't

> IF WHAT YOU BELIEVE DOES NOT CONFORM TO TRUTH, THEN WHAT YOU FEEL DOES NOT CONFORM TO REALITY.

feel loved or saved. It would be safe to say that all of us have had some of our thoughts raised up against the knowledge of God. The good news is that we possess divinely powerful spiritual weapons to tear down mental strongholds (see 2 Cor. 10:3-5).

Truth about God is filtered through the grid of:		
Loving and caring Good and merciful Steadfast and reliable Unconditional grace Present and available Giver of good gifts Nurturing and affirming Accepting Just, fair and impartial	1. Ignorance 2. False prophets and teachers 3. Blasphemous thoughts 4. Unhealthy interpersonal relationships during early developmental years 5. Role model of authority figures—especially parents	Hateful and unconcerned Mean and unforgiving Unpredictable and untrustworthy Conditional approval Absent when needed Takes away, "killjoy" Critical and unpleasable Rejecting Unjust, unfair, partial

Diagram 4.1

Truth without repentance leads to stagnant growth and the inability to experience the freedom that Christ purchased for us on the cross. When our personal and spiritual conflicts are resolved, we connect with God. We know who we are in Christ; the Bible makes sense; and the peace of God, which surpasses all understanding, guards our heart and mind (see Phil. 4:7). When I was able to help the pastor's wife resolve her personal and spiritual conflicts, she emotionally went from the right side of the diagram to the left side.

Paul teaches that our conflicts must be resolved before we can understand God's Word: "I gave you milk to drink, not solid food; for *you were not yet able to receive it*. Indeed, even now you are not yet able, for you are still fleshly. For since there is jealousy and strife among you, are you not fleshly, and are you not walking like mere men?" (1 Cor. 3:2-3, emphasis added). We have observed this all over the world. Christians try to read their Bibles, but the words don't make any sense. They try to pray, but it is like talking to the wall. They hear a message at church, but it goes in one ear and out the other.

Every born-again Christian is a child of God and a new creation in Christ. Incomplete repentance, a lack of faith and unresolved conflicts should not keep us from experiencing our freedom in Christ. This lack of connectedness with God often results in depression. Ultimately, God is our only hope. We must live in harmony with Him if we are going to be free from depression. Those who are severely depressed will need the help and objectivity of a trained encourager. Such was the case of a lady who attended one of my seminars in Europe. She shared the following testimony:

> I was born and raised in a very legalistic and abusive "Christian" home. Church attendance was mandatory, but the physical and emotional abuse I suffered at the

hands of my parents distorted my concept of God. In our church was a large sign that said, "God is love." But I had no idea what love was. If what I experienced at home was supposed to be the love of God, then I wanted no part of it. I moved away from my parents to attend college and away from God. I finished my Ph.D. in psychology and worked as a professional counselor for 20 years. During that time I suffered continuously from depression. Finally I realized that I couldn't help myself much less others, so I went into educational psychology and finally into vocational psychology.

In desperation, I started to attend an international church. A Sunday School class was going through a video series by Neil Anderson. I learned who I was supposed to be in Christ and finally someone explained to me the battle that was going on in my mind. I found out that there were trained encouragers at the church who were taking people through *The Steps to Freedom in Christ*. I made an appointment with great apprehension and much fear. I didn't know what to expect but I knew I had nothing to lose and possibly much to gain.

It was an amazing encounter with God. I could feel the layers of self-righteousness, pride, rebellion and sin come off. Every step was meaningful to me, but the biggest release came when I forgave my parents for their abuse and for distorting my concept of God. As soon as I was done, I knew I was free from years of living in bondage to the lies I believed about God and myself. And I was connected to God in a living and liberating way. His Spirit was now bearing witness with my spirit that I was a child of God. I was set free. I never struggled with depression again.

In our experience, you can win the battle for your mind if you are experiencing your freedom in Christ (i.e., you have no unresolved conflicts between yourself and God). However, if you have many unresolved personal and spiritual conflicts, you can't win the battle. Remember, it is an ongoing battle. Here are some of the most common lies that torment depressed people:

- I'm worthless and would be better off dead.
- I have no value and no meaningful purpose for being here.
- I'll never amount to anything.
- No one loves or cares for me.
- My situation is hopeless; I see no way out but to die.
- I'm stupid; I'm dumb; I'm ugly.
- I'm a mistake.
- God doesn't love me, and He won't help me.
- Life is the pits.
- My future is hopeless.
- Nobody can help me.

Nobody can fix our past—not even God does that. Yet the gospel assures us that we can be free from it. Christians are not primarily products of their pasts. Rather, they are primarily products of Christ's work on the cross and His resurrection. Our primary identity is no longer based on who we were in the flesh; it is based on who we are in Christ. If that were not true, then every Christian would remain a helpless victim of his or her past.

WEED OUT FALSE PERCEPTIONS

Realizing who we are in Christ and what it means to be a child of God is the basis for victorious living and for overcoming depression. No one can consistently behave in a way that is inconsistent with what he or she believes about him- or herself. We will struggle with a poor self-image to the degree that we don't see ourselves the way God sees us. Such negative perceptions of ourselves are based on lies that we have believed. There are several predictable consequences of holding false beliefs about ourselves.

1. False Beliefs Erode Our Confidence and Weaken Our Resolve

Many depressed people think they are losers and choose to believe that they can't do whatever it takes to overcome their problems. If they believe that lie, then they won't take the necessary steps to overcome their depression. Failures fail, losers lose, and sinners sin; but children of God live righteous lives and do all things through Christ who strengthens them. John wrote, "Dear friends, now we are children of God . . . Everyone who has this hope in him purifies himself, just as he is pure" (1 John 3:2-3, NIV). It is not what we do that determines who we are; it is who we are that determines what we do. That is why the Holy Spirit bears witness with our spirit that we are children of God (see Rom. 8:16). "Yet to all who received him, to those who believed in his name, he gave the right to become children of God—children born not of natural descent, nor of human decision or a husband's will, but born of God" (John 1:12-13, NIV).

2. False Beliefs Drive Us to Seek Our Own Acceptance, Security and Significance

People, generally speaking, establish their identity and sense of worth through appearance, performance and social status. No matter how hard we try, we will still suffer from morbid introspection, hostile criticism, overt rejection and endless accusations. That is depressing! Acceptance, security and significance are already met because of our relationship with God. Defeated

Christians strive for what they already have in Christ, desperately trying to become someone they already are. "As you come to him, the living Stone—rejected by men but chosen by God and precious to him—you also, like living stones, are being built into a spiritual house to be a holy priesthood" (1 Pet. 2:4-5, *NIV*).

3. False Beliefs Precipitate a Fear of Failure
To stumble and fall is not failure. To stumble and fall again is not failure. Failure comes when we say we were pushed. There are no unforgivable failures in the kingdom of God, but there are many who live far below their potential because they have never learned the truth of who they are in Christ: "There is now no condemnation for those who are *in Christ Jesus*" (Rom. 8:1, *NIV*, emphasis added). We probably learn more from our mistakes than we will ever learn from our successes. A mistake is only a failure when you fail to learn from it: "For though a righteous man falls seven times, he rises again" (Prov. 24:16, *NIV*). If you make a mistake, get back up and try again and again and again. This is not a question of self-confidence. Our confidence is in God. Paul says, "We who worship by the Spirit of God, who glory in Christ Jesus, and who put no confidence in the flesh" (Phil. 3:3, *NIV*).

4. False Beliefs Cause Us to Seek the Approval and Affirmation of Others
The need for affirmation and approval is universal. So great is the need that it should draw us to our heavenly Father, because we are not going to have that need perfectly met in this world no matter how hard we try. Jesus lived a perfect life, and everyone rejected Him. Yet He had the approval of His heavenly Father. Paul asks, "Am I now trying to win the approval of men, or of God? Or am I trying to please men? If I were still trying to please men, I would not be a servant of Christ" (Gal. 1:10, *NIV*). We will

be servants of humankind instead of God if we try to win people's approval and seek their affirmation.

We don't do the things we do with the hope that God may someday accept us. We already have His approval and affirmation in Christ, which is why we do the things we do. We don't labor in the vineyard with the hope that someday God may love us. We already have God's unconditional love since we are His children. That is why we labor in the vineyard.

Scripture warns us not to exalt ourselves (see Luke 14:7-11) and to be aware of those who stroke our egos: "For such people are not serving our Lord Christ, but their own appetites. By smooth talk and flattery they deceive the minds of naive people" (Rom. 16:18, *NIV*). Paul's written exhortation to the Thessalonians and to us reminds us to be less concerned about the opinions of others and more concerned about what God thinks: "We are not trying to please men but God, who tests our hearts. You know we never used flattery, nor did we put on a mask to cover up greed—God is our witness. We were not looking for praise from men, not from you or anyone else" (1 Thess. 2:4-6, *NIV*).

5. False Beliefs Rob Us of the Courage to Stand Up for Our Convictions and Beliefs

A person with a low sense of worth thinks, *My opinions don't matter. If I share what I really believe, others will only squash me.* Caving in to the fear of rejection undermines the courage to stand up for our convictions. Depressed people frequently think of themselves as weak or cowardly.

6. False Beliefs Lead to Codependent Relationships

Christians are interdependent in a healthy sense, because we absolutely need God, and we necessarily need each other. Plus, we are under the conviction of God to love one another (i.e., meet one another's needs). It becomes unhealthy, however, when we believe that, *I can't live without you, your acceptance or your approval.* It is equally unhealthy if we let a sick person dictate to us how we love them.

7. False Beliefs Make It Difficult to Receive Ordinary Compliments

Affirmations, praises and compliments do not remove the terrible pain that depressed people feel. Because their pain does not go away, they conclude (wrongly) that expressions of praise or gratitude are not genuine. Acceptance and affirmation accomplishes more when directed toward these people's character rather than their appearance, performance or social status, and when it reinforces who they really are in Christ. On the other hand, rejection and criticism of any kind contribute to their depressed state, because these negative attitudes match existing false beliefs. Suspicions are confirmed when we put down rather than build up a depressed person.

RECOGNIZE ASSIMILATED ATTITUDES

People do not come into this world with a built-in sense of worth, nor do they inherently feel good about themselves. Without God's presence in their lives, they try to derive those basic needs from the world. Nobody had perfect parents, but according to Dr. Gary Collins, children rarely are damaged by the minor errors all parents make. Real feelings of inferiority emerge when parents:

1. criticize, shame, reject and punish repeatedly
2. set unrealistic standards and goals
3. express the expectation that the child will fail
4. punish repeatedly and harshly

5. avoid cuddling, hugging or affectionate touching
6. imply that children are a nuisance, stupid or incompetent
7. overprotect or dominate children so that they fail later when forced to be on their own[2]

DISCARD INADEQUATE SOLUTIONS

I can't think of a topic that produces more distortions and inadequate solutions than establishing our identity and building self-esteem. "Non-Christian counselors and therapists emphasize restoring a healthy self-image, building self-esteem and enhancing self-worth. This sounds good on the surface. Closer examination, however, reveals that the secular mindset sometimes produces a person who is self-satisfied, self-indulgent sexually and self-reliant apart from God."[3] Picking ourselves up by our own bootstraps and stroking one another's egos is not going to get it done. "America is besieged by a low sense of worth. Rather than seeking quick fix solutions from pop psychologists, we ought to encourage people to seek their sense of worth through Christ. Imagine the consequences if we could get people to understand that their value is not self-determined, but has already been determined for them by God."[4]

Even among Christians we hear many inadequate solutions for attaining our identity and sense of worth. It has been suggested that men get their identity from their work and women from bearing children. Perhaps some see that in Genesis 3, where it states that women shall bear their children in pain and men shall work by the sweat of their brows (see vv. 16, 19). But that is a fallen identity. What happens if a man loses his job? Does he lose his identity? What happens if a woman never marries or can't have children? Does she lose her identity? Who we are has already been established by God in creation and redemption. What name could you make for yourself that would be better than calling yourself a child of God (see John 1:12)?

Do we get a sense of worth from spiritual gifts? No! Right in the middle of the most definitive teaching on spiritual gifts, Paul wrote, "Those members of the body which we deem less honorable, on these we bestow more abundant honor, and our less presentable members become much more presentable, whereas our more presentable members have no need of it. But God has so composed the body, giving more abundant honor to that member which lacked" (1 Cor. 12:23-24).

Do we get our sense of worth from talents? No! God has given some people one talent, others two talents and others five talents (see Matt. 25:14). *God, how could you do that? Don't you know, Lord, that only people with five talents can have any legitimate sense of worth?* That is not true. In fact, supergifted and supertalented people often struggle more since they often establish their identity and sense of worth in gifts and talents, which can distract them from developing their character and relationship with God—from where true identity and fulfillment comes.

Does our sense of worth come from intelligence? No! "God has chosen the foolish things of the world to shame the wise" (1 Cor. 1:27). God has not equally distributed gifts, talents or intelligence. He has equally distributed Himself. Only in Christ is there equality: "You are all sons of God through faith in Christ Jesus. For all of you who were baptized into Christ have clothed yourselves with Christ. There is neither Jew nor Greek, there is neither slave nor free man, there is neither male nor female; for you are all one in Christ Jesus. And if you belong to Christ, then you are Abraham's descendants, heirs according to promise" (Gal. 3:26-29).

Perhaps the most fickle of all false foundations are appearance, performance and social status. Fallen humanity labors under the following false equations:

1. Appearance + Admiration = A Whole Person
2. Performance + Accomplishments = A Whole Person
3. Social Status + Recognition = A Whole Person

Recognition is not the same as acceptance, and the respect given by others may be based more on position and possession than on the character of an individual. No matter how hard you try, someone will come along and look or perform better. Talents and appearances fade with time. When you strive for the acceptance, recognition or admiration of others, then it is they who determine your worth. If they judge you unworthy, are you then worthless? What a tragedy to put your identity and sense of worth in someone else's hands. Who will judge your worth? Who declares you to have value? Can one pot declare to another pot its true worth? Only the potter has the right to determine who you are. The value He placed on your life cost Him His only begotten Son. You plus Christ makes you a whole person. You are now complete in Christ (see Col. 3:10).

There is certainly nothing wrong with gifts, talents, intelligence, appearance, performance and social status rightly achieved. They are life endowments given to us by our creator, of which we are to be good stewards. If someone gave us a new car, we would not find our identity and sense of worth in the car. The giver of the car found value in us, which is why he or she gave us the car. There are no strings attached to the gift, but we would want to use the car in such a way as to show appreciation for the gift. To abuse the free gift would be to dishonor the giver.

CHOOSE THE ONLY ANSWER

Although Peter was addressing wives, we believe the following applies to all of God's children:

Your beauty should not come from outward adornment, such as braided hair and the wearing of gold jewelry and fine clothes. Instead, it should be that of your inner self, the unfading beauty of a gentle and quiet spirit, which is of great worth in God's sight (1 Pet. 3:3-4, *NIV*).

Our identity and sense of worth come from knowing who we are as children of God and becoming the person He created us to be. Nobody nor anything on planet Earth can keep us from being who He created us to be—that is God's will for our lives. "For this is the will of God, your sanctification" (1 Thess. 4:3).

If Christians knew who they were in Christ and if their lives were characterized by love, joy, peace, patience, kindness, goodness, faithfulness, gentleness and self-control, would they feel good about themselves? Of course they would. Who can possess these qualities? Every child of God has exactly the same opportunity. It is the fruit of the Spirit (see Gal. 5:22-23), of which every Christian is a partaker. Such characteristics cannot come by way of the world, the flesh or the devil. They can only come by abiding in Christ and walking by faith according to what God says is true in the power of the Holy Spirit.

Paul said, "My God will supply all your needs according to His riches in glory in Christ Jesus" (Phil. 4:19). The most critical needs are the "being" needs, and they are the ones most wonderfully met in Christ. The greatest need is life itself, and Jesus came that we might have life (i.e., spiritual life). The Holy Spirit settles the identity problem when He bears witness with our spirit that we are children of God. In order to be accepted, secure and significant, we need to turn to God—and only God. I tried to show how the being needs are met in Christ in my book *Who I Am in Christ* (Regal Books, 2001). The following outline from the book not only reveals who we are in Christ, but how those needs are met:

IN CHRIST

I Am Accepted in Christ

John 1:12	I am God's child.
John 15:15	I am Christ's friend.
Romans 5:1	I have been justified.
1 Corinthians 6:17	I am united with the Lord, and I am one with Him in spirit.
1 Corinthians 6:19-20	I have been bought with a price. I belong to God.
1 Corinthians 12:27	I am a member of Christ's Body.
Ephesians 1:1	I am a saint.
Ephesians 1:5	I have been adopted as God's child.
Ephesians 2:18	I have direct access to God through the Holy Spirit.
Colossians 1:14	I have been redeemed and forgiven of all my sins.
Colossians 2:10	I am complete in Christ.

I Am Secure in Christ

Romans 8:1-2	I am free from condemnation.
Romans 8:28	I am assured that all things work together for good.
Romans 8:31-34	I am free from any condemning charges against me.
Romans 8:35-39	I cannot be separated from the love of God.
2 Corinthians 1:21-22	I have been established, anointed and sealed by God.
Philippians 1:6	I am confident that the good work God has begun in me will be perfected.

Philippians 3:20	I am a citizen of heaven.
Colossians 3:3	I am hidden with Christ in God.
2 Timothy 1:7	I have not been given a spirit of fear but of power, love and a sound mind.
Hebrews 4:16	I can find grace and mercy to help in times of need.
1 John 5:18	I am born of God and the evil one cannot touch me.

I Am Significant in Christ

Matthew 5:13-14	I am the salt and light of the earth.
John 15:1,5	I am a branch of the true vine, a channel of His life.
John 15:16	I have been chosen and appointed to bear fruit.
Acts 1:8	I am a personal witness of Christ.
1 Corinthians 3:16	I am God's temple.
2 Corinthians 5:17-21	I am a minister of reconciliation for God.
2 Corinthians 6:1	I am God's coworker.
Ephesians 2:6	I am seated with Christ in the heavenly realm.
Ephesians 2:10	I am God's workmanship.
Ephesians 3:12	I may approach God with freedom and confidence.
Philippians 4:13	I can do all things through Christ who strengthens me.

To sense divine grace—the Christian parallel to psychology's "unconditional positive regard"—is to be liberated from both self-protective pride and self-condemnation. To feel profoundly affirmed, just as we are, lessens our need to define our self-worth in terms of achievements, prestige or material and physical well-being. It is like insecure Pinocchio saying to his maker, Geppetto, "Papa, I am not sure who I am. But if I'm all right with you, then I guess I'm all right with me."[5]

CHAPTER FIVE

OVERCOMING HOPELESSNESS

Why are you downcast, O my soul? Why so disturbed within me? Put your hope in God, for I will yet praise him, my Savior and my God.

PSALM 43:5, *NIV*

A newly adopted child found himself in a big mansion. His new Father whispered in his ear, "This is yours and you have a right to be here. I have made you a joint heir with My only begotten Son. He paid the price that set you free from your old taskmaster, who was cruel and condemning. I purchased it for you, because I love you." The young boy couldn't help but question this incredible gift, *It seems too good to be true. What did I do to deserve this?* he wondered. *I have been a slave all my life, and I have done nothing to earn such a privilege!*

He was deeply grateful, however, and began to explore all the rooms in the mansion. He tried out some of the tools and appliances. There were many other people in the mansion who also had been adopted. He began to form new relationships with his adopted brothers and sisters. He especially enjoyed the buffet table from which he freely ate. Then it happened! While turning away from the buffet table, he knocked over a stack of glasses and a valuable pitcher that crashed to the floor and broke. Suddenly he began to think, *You clumsy, stupid kid! You will never get away with this. What right do you have to be here? You had better hide before someone finds out, because they will surely throw you out.*

At first he was caught up in the wonder of living in the mansion with a whole new family and a loving Father, but now he was confused. Old memories from early childhood began to replay in his mind. He was filled with guilt and shame. *Who do you think you are? Some kind of privileged character? You don't belong here anymore; you belong in the basement! The old taskmaster was right about me, I don't belong here.* So he descended into the basement.

The cellar was dreary, dark and despairing. The only light came from the open door at the crest of the long stairs. He heard his Father calling for him, but he was too ashamed to answer. He was surprised to find others in the basement. Upstairs everybody talked to each other and particpated in fun and meaningful daily projects. Nobody talked to each other in the basement. They were too ashamed. Most basement dwellers felt that they really belonged in the basement anyway.

Those in the basement didn't like the basement, but they didn't see how they could ever walk in the light again. If they did, others would see their imperfections. Old friends occasionally came to the door and encouraged them to return upstairs where a place was prepared for them. Some "friends" were worse than others and scolded those in the basement, which only made it worse. Not everybody stayed in the basement for the same reason. Some thought like the child did, *I deserve to be here. I was given a chance, but I blew it.* Others didn't think they could climb the stairs. Even if they mustered up the strength to try, the stairs would probably break under their weight. They always had a reason why they couldn't return to their Father upstairs. Some would return for a short time, but they didn't stay long enough to resolve their conflicts and learn the truth that would enable them to stay. So they returned. Still others were afraid that they would not be accepted. Their old taskmaster didn't accept them, so how could they expect this adoptive parent to welcome them back after what they had done?

At first, the newly adopted child groped around in the darkness, trying to find a way to survive. The longer he stayed in the basement, the more his memory of living upstairs began to fade, and so did his hope of ever returning. Those old childhood memories questioned the love of this new Father, and he began to question whether he was ever adopted in the first place. The noise of people having fun upstairs irritated him. He remembered the light upstairs being warm and inviting, but now it was penetrating and revealing. He recalled hearing his adopted Father say, "Men loved darkness instead of light because their deeds were evil. Everyone who does evil hates the light, and will not come into the light for fear that his deeds will be exposed" (John 3:19-20, *NIV*).

He made a few halfhearted attempts to return to the light, but eventually he found a dark corner to lie down in. To survive he ate grubs and moss off the damp walls. Then one day a shaft of light penetrated his mind and reason returned. He began to think, *Why not throw myself on the mercy of this person who calls Himself my Father? What do I have to lose? Even if He makes me eat the crumbs that fall from the table, it would be better than this.* He decided to take the risk of climbing those stairs and face his Father with the truth of what he had done. "Lord," he said, "I knocked over some glasses and broke a pitcher." Without saying a word, his Father took him by the hand and led him into the dining room. To his utter amazement his Father had prepared for him a banquet. "Welcome home," his Father said. "There is now no condemnation for those who are in Christ Jesus" (Rom. 8:1, *NIV*).

Oh the deep, deep love of Jesus, and the matchless grace of God. The door is always open for those who are willing to throw themselves upon the mercy of God. "In love he predestined us to be adopted as his sons through Jesus Christ, in accordance with His pleasure and will—to the praise of his glorious grace, which he has freely given us in the One he loves" (Eph. 1:4-6, *NIV*). God doesn't want us to live self-condemned in the basement. He wants us to know that we are seated with Christ in the heavenlies as joint heirs with Jesus: "Now if we are children, then we are heirs—heirs of God and coheirs with Christ, if indeed we share in his sufferings in order that we may also share in his glory" (Rom. 8:17, *NIV*).

ACCEPT GOD'S GRACE

How does someone understand the grace of God? How can *anyone* fully understand the love and grace of God? Everything we learn in the world teaches us otherwise. Living a natural life on this planet is hazardous, and only those who are mentally, emotionally and physically fit will survive; and justice demands that we get what we deserve. "But when the kindness and love of God our Savior appeared, he saved us, not because of righteous things we had done, but because of his mercy" (Titus 3:4-5, *NIV*).

Inspired by the Holy Spirit, Paul offers two prayers in the book of Ephesians. He first petitions God to open our eyes to who we are and the rich inheritance that we have in Christ: "I pray also that the eyes of your heart may be enlightened in order that you may know the hope to which he has called you, the riches of his glorious inheritance in the saints, and his incomparably great power for us who believe" (Eph. 1:18-19, *NIV*).

In the second prayer he petitions God on our behalf. Personalize this prayer by putting your name in the allotted space:

> *For this reason I kneel before the Father, from whom His whole family in heaven and on Earth derives its name. I pray that out of His glorious riches He may strengthen _____ with power through His Spirit in _____ inner being, so that Christ may dwell in _____ heart through faith. And I pray that _____, being rooted and established in love, may have power, together with all the saints, to grasp how wide and long and high and deep is the love of Christ, and to know this love that surpasses knowledge—that _____ may be filled to the measure of all the fullness of God [see Eph. 3:14-19].*

Nonbelievers are guilty before a holy God, and there is nothing they can do about it. Every attempt to live a righteous life in their own strength will fail. But the penalty for every born-again Christian's sin has been paid in full. We may feel a psychological guilt when we do something that violates our conscience—the mind. However, psychological guilt is not the same thing as the convicting work of the Holy Spirit. Even nonbelievers have a conscience, and they feel shame or guilt when it is violated. The process of renewing the mind will bring the believer's conscience in conformity to the nature and character of God.

When the devil first tempts us to sin, he quickly changes his role and becomes the accuser. *You will never get away with this. How can you even consider yourself a Christian if you do those kinds of things?*

The Lord has forgiven our sins and defeated the devil as Paul so clearly revealed:

> When you were dead in your sins and in the uncircumcision of your sinful nature, God made you alive with Christ. He forgave us all our sins, having canceled the written code, with its regulations, that was against us and that stood opposed to us; he took it away, nailing it to the cross. And having disarmed the powers and authorities, he made a public spectacle of them, triumphing over them by the cross (Col. 2:13-15, *NIV*).

The Lord will not tempt us, but He will test us in order to perfect our faith. He will also convict us of sin in order to cleanse us from all unrighteousness. How then do we know the difference between the convicting work of the Holy Spirit and the accusations of the devil or a condemning conscience that has been programmed by the world? Paul answers this question in 2 Corinthians 7:9-11 (*NIV*), "Now I am happy, not because you were made sorry, but because your sorrow led you to repentance. For you became sorrowful as God intended and so were not harmed in any way by us. Godly sorrow brings repentance that leads to salvation and leaves no regret, but worldly sorrow brings death."

The word "sorrow" is used to describe both the conviction of God and the false guilt produced by the world, the flesh and the devil. In other words, conviction and false guilt may feel the same, but the end result is totally different. The conviction of God leads to repentance without regret. This is a wonderful truth that we have witnessed numerous times. I have never seen anyone regret going through *The Steps to Freedom in Christ* in order to resolve personal and spiritual conflicts through repentance and faith in God. What stays with people after they have gone through The Steps is the freedom they experience, not the pain from the past. Their past pain was nailed to the Cross. Peter betrayed Christ by denying Him three times. Later he came under the conviction of the Holy Spirit and became the spokesperson for the Early Church. Judas betrayed Christ. Later he came under the sorrow of the world and hung himself.

REJECT HOPELESSNESS'S LIES

The hopelessness that accompanies depression was aptly described by one woman who said, "It feels like I am in a well 1,000 feet deep. From the bottom I look up and see a faint light the size of a pin-hole. I have no ladder, no rope and no way out." Depression is hopelessness based on a lie. With God there is always hope based on truth. According to Hebrews 6:13-20 (*NIV*), God stakes His own credibility on the fact that our hope is in Him:

> When God made his promise to Abraham, since there was no one greater for him to swear by, he swore by himself, saying, "I will surely bless you and give you many descendants." And so after waiting patiently, Abraham received what was promised. Men swear by someone greater than themselves, and the oath confirms what is said and puts an end to all argument. Because God wanted to make the unchanging nature of his purpose very clear to the heirs of what was promised, he confirmed it with an oath. God did this so that, by two unchangeable things in which it is impossible for God to lie, we who have fled to take hold of the hope offered to us may be greatly encouraged. We have this hope as an anchor for the soul, firm and secure. It enters the inner sanctuary behind the curtain, where Jesus, who went before us, has entered on our behalf.

The two unchangeable things are God's promise and the oath confirming His promise. Our hope in God is the anchor for our soul and the answer for depression. If God cannot lie, then the basis for our hope is found in the truth of His nature, character and Word. God cannot change, but our perception of Him can, which can greatly affect how we feel. To illustrate this, look at Jeremiah who is depressed because of his skewed perceptions about God:

> I am the man who has seen affliction because of the rod of His wrath. He has driven me and made me walk in darkness and not in light. Surely against me He has turned His hand repeatedly all the day. He has caused my flesh and my skin to waste away, He has broken my bones. He has besieged and encompassed me with bitterness and hardship. In dark places He has made me dwell, like those who have long been dead (Lam. 3:1-6).

Jeremiah believes that God is the cause of his physical and emotional hardships. He actually believes that God is out to get him when in fact God is out to restore him. Instead of being led by God, he feels like he is being driven to dark places where God has abandoned him. Jeremiah is in the basement! Consider his feelings of entrapment, hopelessness and fear:

> He has walled me in so that I cannot go out; He has made my chain heavy. Even when I cry out and call for help, He shuts out my prayer. He has blocked my ways with hewn stone; He has made my paths crooked. He is to me like a bear lying in wait, like a lion in secret places. He has turned aside my ways and torn me to pieces; He has made me desolate. So I say, "My strength has perished, and so has my hope from the LORD" (Lam. 3:7-11,18).

Jeremiah was depressed because his perception of God was wrong. God wasn't the cause of his affliction. God didn't set up the circumstances to make his life miserable. God is not a wild beast waiting to chew people up, but Jeremiah thought He was and consequently lost his hope in God. Yet suddenly everything changed:

> I remember my affliction and my wandering, the bitterness and the gall. I well remember them, and my soul is downcast within me. Yet this I call to mind and therefore I have hope: Because of the LORD's great love we are not consumed, for his compassions never fail. They are new every morning; great is your faithfulness. I say to myself, "The LORD is my portion; therefore I will wait for him." The LORD is good to those whose hope is in him, to the one who seeks him; it is good to wait quietly for the salvation of the LORD (Lam. 3:19-26, *NIV*).

Nothing changed externally in Jeremiah's experience—the only thing that changed was his acknowledgment of God. He won the battle for his mind by recalling what he knew to be true about God. Hope returns when we choose to believe the true nature and character of God, which is why it is so necessary for us to worship God. Our heavenly Father doesn't need us to tell Him who He is. We worship God because we need to constantly keep the divine attributes of God on our mind.

The writer of Hebrews said, "Faith is being sure of what we hope for and certain of what we do not see" (11:1, *NIV*). Martin Luther said, "Everything that is done in the world is done in hope. No husbandman would sow one grain of corn if he hoped not it would grow up and become seed; no bachelor would marry a wife if he hoped not to have children; no merchant or tradesman would set himself to work if he did not hope to reap benefit thereby."[1]

Hope can be illustrated in many practical ways. Suppose you hope to catch the next bus scheduled at 11:00 A.M. You leave your home at 10:45 A.M., giving yourself enough time to walk at a leisurely pace. You walk by faith to the bus stop with the hope that the bus is on time and that the schedule is right. Your hope will be dashed if the bus is late or the schedule is wrong. You will lose faith in the public transportation system. And if you fall behind schedule and think you have no hope of catching the next bus, you will not proceed by faith. That would be foolish. What if you believed there was no hope of being loved, no hope of eternal life, no hope of change, no hope for the future or no hope for joy in your life? You would probably be depressed and not very willing to continue living by faith.

> OUR HOPE IN GOD IS THE
> ANCHOR FOR OUR SOUL AND THE
> ANSWER FOR DEPRESSION.

Biblical hope is not wishful thinking. Hope is the present assurance of some future good based on the true nature and character of God. Remember, our hope is in God, not in humanity and the circumstances of life. His Word is true. His promises can be counted on and claimed with confidence. He cannot break His New Covenant that assures us of His presence within us and the forgiveness of our sins (see Heb. 8:8-13). Matthew Henry said, "The ground of our hope is Christ in the world, but the evidence of our hope is Christ in the Heart."[2] "To them God has chosen to make known among the Gentiles the glorious riches of this mystery, which is Christ in you, the hope of glory" (Col. 1:27, *NIV*). It is His presence within us that changes our mood and perception of reality: "Why are you in despair, O my soul? And why have you become disturbed within me? Hope in God, for I shall again praise Him for the help of His presence" (Ps. 42:5).

SEEK GOD'S TRUTH

A sense of hopelessness is an emotional reaction to how we perceive ourselves, the circumstances surrounding us and the future. The resultant emotional state is not based on reality, or perceived truthfully from God's perspective. Someone once said that life with Christ is an endless hope, but life without Christ is a hopeless end. The world is filled with naysayers, negative circumstances and obstacles we often don't see. Hope is the parent of faith, the evidence of things not seen. Biblical hope must be established and maintained if we are going to experience freedom from depression. To guide us through the maze of life, we must know the truth of God's Word and be led by the Holy Spirit.

It seems easier to throw in the towel when our health is failing and the circumstances are negative. One of the most common characteristics of burnout is the loss of hope.[3] Unless we want to be depressed, it is essential to maintain our hope when facing difficult circumstances. Nehemiah was called by God to rebuild the protective walls around Jerusalem. In addition to facing seemingly insurmountable odds, Nehemiah was jeered by Sanballat and Tobiah who set out to create a sense of hopelessness:

> When Sanballat heard that we were rebuilding the wall, he became angry and was greatly incensed. He ridiculed the Jews, and in the presence of his associates and the army of Samaria, he said, "What are those feeble Jews doing? Will they restore their wall? Will they

offer sacrifices? Will they finish in a day? Can they bring the stones back to life from those heaps of rubble—burned as they are?" Tobiah the Ammonite, who was at his side, said, "What they are building—if even a fox climbed up on it, he would break down their wall of stones!" (Neh. 4:1-3, *NIV*).

Have you ever been in a seemingly impossible situation where the voices from your enemies (or in your mind) ridiculed your efforts? What did Nehemiah do? He prayed, posted a guard and kept working (see vv. 9-23). Nehemiah was successful in rebuilding the walls, but the enemy never gave up. He just changed strategies. His enemies saw one chink in the armor, but Nehemiah was up for the challenge:

When word came to Sanballat, Tobiah, Geshem the Arab and the rest of our enemies that I had rebuilt the wall and not a gap was left in it—though up to that time I had not set the doors in the gates—Sanballat and Geshem sent me this message: "Come, let us meet together in one of the villages on the plain of Ono." But they were scheming to harm me; so I sent messengers to them with this reply: "I am carrying on a great project and cannot go down. Why should the work stop while I leave it and go down to you?" Four times they sent me the same message, and each time I gave them the same answer (6:1-4, *NIV*).

The devil is persistent, but we must never let him set the agenda. We don't negotiate with the enemy, nor do we let him distract us from our calling in life. In the face of opposition, our answer is always the same: I am a child of God, saved by the blood of the Lord Jesus Christ, and I choose to live my life by faith according to what God says is true in the power of the Holy Spirit.

In this world we are going to face negative circumstances and inevitable losses. Our hope does not lie in our ability to overcome these obstacles with our own strength and resources but with God's strength and resources. Nor does our hope lie in the eternal preservation of our physical body. Our ultimate hope lies in the resurrection: "Therefore, since through God's mercy we have this ministry, we do not lose heart. Rather, we have renounced secret and shameful ways; we do not use deception, nor do we distort the word of God. On the contrary, by setting forth the truth plainly we commend ourselves to every man's conscience in the sight of God" (2 Cor. 4:1-2, *NIV*). Paul then shows how we do not lose hope in the midst of negative circumstances and failing health:

> But we have this treasure in jars of clay to show that this all-surpassing power is from God and not from us. We are hard pressed on every side, but not crushed; perplexed, but not in despair; persecuted, but not abandoned; struck down, but not destroyed. We always carry around in our body the death of Jesus, so that the life of Jesus may also be revealed in our body. For we who are alive are always being given over to death for Jesus' sake, so that his life may be revealed in our mortal body. Therefore we do not lose heart. Though outwardly we are wasting away, yet inwardly we are being renewed day by day. For our light and momentary troubles are achieving for us an eternal glory that far outweighs them all. So we fix our eyes not on what is seen, but on what is unseen. For what is seen is temporary, but what is unseen is eternal (2 Cor. 4:7-11,16-18, *NIV*).

Dr. Victor Frankl, an Austrian psychiatrist, observed that a prisoner did not live very long after hope was lost. Yet even the slightest ray of hope—the rumor of better food, a whisper about an escape—helped some of the camp inmates to continue living even under systematic horror.[4] There is not enough darkness in all the world to put out the light of one small candle. Truth always shines through the darkness. We close this chapter with a testimony of how light shining in the darkness set a captive free:

> I was raised in a good family and had a very good child-hood. I received Christ into my life when I was 20 and married a Christian woman when I was 22. We had three children and I worked in the same excavating business that my father and grandfather owned.
>
> When I was 31, I decided to start my own business. The first two years went great and life seemed to be very good. In the third spring of my new business, I learned that my mother had Lou Gehrig's disease, which has no known cure. That spring was incredibly wet, which made it almost impossible to get any work done. The bills piled up and for the first time in my life I started to feel depressed.
>
> I always felt that I was in control of my life, but now everything I did seemed to make it worse. I felt guilty that I couldn't be with my mother, who lived 800 miles away. We fell further behind in our bills, and then my wife suffered a miscarriage. It seemed like I had lost con-trol of everything. The depression got worse and I start-ed to think of suicide.
>
> The next season I started so far behind that I didn't see any way to catch up with my bills, and my mother was get-ting worse. The fact that she wasn't a Christian weighed heavily on me. Then, praise God, my father led himself and my mother to Christ. Finally, something good happened. A short time later she died, and I still miss her.

When the bill collectors called, all I could think of was to kill myself. I could sense no hope. In the past I could always fix things, but now I couldn't. I finally decided to end it all. On my way out to get a gun, two questions came to my mind. First, *Which is more important, having your bills paid by the insurance money or your children having a father?* Second, *Which is more important, having your bills paid or your wife having a husband?* At that moment I knew I didn't want to kill myself, but those condemning and suicidal thoughts just wouldn't go away.

I met with my pastor regularly, but I still couldn't see any hope. Then I met with a friend who had gone to a Living Free in Christ conference. He showed me in Ephesians 1:18-21 that I have Christ in me and the same power that raised Him from the dead. He asked me if I thought there was anything that power couldn't do. Of course not! He then explained how the battle was in my mind and how I could win that battle by taking every thought captive to the obedience of Christ. From that time on, I have not been depressed or entertained any thoughts of suicide. I finally found the hope I had been looking for.

A few weeks later, my friend moved away. There was so much more that I wanted to learn, so I bought *Victory over the Darkness* and *The Bondage Breaker*. I read them both on my way to Washington, D.C., to attend the Promise Keepers event "Stand in the Gap." The transformation has been incredible. My wife tells me she has a new husband. When I read God's Word, it comes alive. When I listen to my pastor preach, I often cry because the Word of God touches my heart. My life will never be the same because of the freedom that Christ has given me.

OVERCOMING
HELPLESSNESS

*The pain is unrelenting, and what makes the condition intolerable is the foreknowl-
edge that no remedy will come—not in a day, an hour, a month, or a minute.
If there is mild relief, one knows that it is only temporary; more pain will follow. It is
hopelessness even more than the pain that crushes the soul. So the decision-making of
daily life involves not, as in normal affairs, shifting from one annoying situation to
another less annoying—or from discomfort to relative comfort, or from boredom to
activity—but moving from pain to pain. One does not abandon, even briefly, one's
bed of nails, but is attached to it wherever one goes.*

WILLIAM STYRON, *DARKNESS VISIBLE: A MEMOIR OF MADNESS*

People who struggle with depression frequently complain
about feelings of helplessness. They can point to a series of life

circumstances over which they had no control. These often include job loss, serious illness or injury, death of a loved one or divorce. Some aspects of these situations were in fact beyond their ability to control. Because they have no control over certain events, they start to believe that they are inadequate, incompetent and powerless. Consequently, they feel helpless, even though Scripture says they can do all things through Christ, who strengthens them (see Phil. 4:13). The belief that they are unable to affect their world or to keep from being affected by the world has overtaken them! Helplessness creeps in when we don't know or fail to believe the truth. It is something we have learned; therefore, helplessness is something that must be unlearned.

LEARNED HELPLESSNESS

Dr. Martin Seligman, a researcher, conducted experiments that linked helplessness with depression.[1] He constructed an environment where a dog was administered a shock in a kennel and could not escape it by jumping or hiding. Dogs that endured this treatment learned that they were helpless. Nothing that the dog tried reduced the pain. These dogs were conditioned to accept the shock as an inevitable consequence of living!

Seligman then demonstrated that dogs exposed to this treatment had more trouble avoiding an escapable shock than dogs not previously conditioned to such training. Additionally, the dogs conditioned to the shock treatment developed the characteristics of depression. They had difficulty eating, sleeping and self-grooming. They moved slower and appeared less alert.

Many other experiments have revealed the same thing. In one experiment, fleas were put in a jar with a piece of glass on the top. If a flea made any attempt to leave the jar, it only bumped into the glass. It didn't take long to condition the fleas to believe that they could not leave the jar. When the glass top was removed, they never even tried to leave because they were conditioned to believe that they could not.

In another experiment, a glass divider was placed inside a fish tank with all the fish on one side. Food was put on the other side of the divider. After repeatedly bumping into the glass, the fish no longer tried to get the food. When the glass divider was removed, the fish remained on their side of the tank.

Have you ever gone to a circus and noticed an elephant that was staked to the ground? How could that little stake keep that big elephant immobilized? It couldn't, but the elephant didn't know that. When elephants are very young and physically weak, they are staked to the ground. As they grow older and bigger, they can easily dislodge the stake; but they don't believe that they can, so they don't even try. They are conditioned to stop trying when they meet the slightest resistance.

HELPLESS PEOPLE

Helplessness is a distortion of the truth. Scripture has illustrations of learned helplessness. The Israelites had been enslaved to Egypt for 400 years when God revealed to Moses His plans to set them free:

> Therefore, say to the Israelites: "I am the LORD, and I will bring you out from under the yoke of the Egyptians. I will free you from being slaves to them, and I will redeem you with an outstretched arm and with mighty acts of judgment. I will take you as my own people, and I will be your God. Then you will know that I am the LORD your God, who brought you out from under the yoke of the Egyptians. And I will bring you to the land I swore with uplifted hand to give to Abraham, to Isaac and to Jacob. I will give it to you as a possession. I am the LORD" (Exod. 6:6-8, *NIV*).

Pack your bags, Israelites! God is about to open the prison doors and set the captive free. He knows your plight. He loves you and wants to redeem you and bring you back to the Promised Land! Listen, however, to the Israelites's response to this good news: "Moses reported this to the Israelites, but they did not listen to him because of their discouragement and cruel bondage" (v. 9, *NIV*). Years of conditioning created a sense of learned helplessness even when God Himself said He would deliver them. When God did deliver the Israelites from Egypt, they stalled in the wilderness. The people became greatly discouraged and wanted to go back. They rebelled and complained about Moses' leadership. About this time, "The LORD said to Moses, 'Send some men to explore the land of Canaan, which I am giving to the Israelites. From each ancestral tribe send one of its leaders'" (Num. 13:1-2, *NIV*). The leaders then returned to Moses and Aaron and the whole Israelite community and gave this report:

> "We went into the land to which you sent us, and it does flow with milk and honey! Here is its fruit. But the people who live there are powerful, and the cities are fortified and very large. We even saw descendants of Anak there." Then Caleb silenced the people before Moses and said, "We should go up and take possession of the land, for we can certainly do it." But the men who had gone up with him said, "We can't attack those people; they are stronger than we are." And they spread among the Israelites a bad report about the land they had explored. They said, "The land we explored devours those living in it. All the people we saw there are of great size. We saw the Nephilim there (the descendants of Anak come from the Nephilim). We seemed like grasshoppers *in our own eyes*, and we looked the same to them" (vv. 27-28,30-33, *NIV*, emphasis added).

The people believed the bad report and rebelled against Moses and Aaron. But Joshua and Caleb said to the entire Israelite assembly:

> The land we passed through and explored is exceedingly good. If the LORD is pleased with us, he will lead us into that land, a land flowing with milk and honey, and will give it to us. Only do not rebel against the LORD. And do not be afraid of the people of the land, because we will swallow them up. Their protection is gone, but the LORD is with us. Do not be afraid of them (Num. 14:7-9, *NIV*).

Unfortunately, the Israelites believed the bad report, not the truth. The Lord delivered them into the Promised Land anyway, but because of their disobedience, they wandered the wilderness for another 40 years. After they arrived in the Promised Land, they still encountered many obstacles (as we will today).

One such obstacle was the Philistines, who challenged the Israelites to a winner-take-all match between their champion, Goliath, and anyone the Israelites chose. The Israelites were paralyzed by fear until David came along and said, "Who is this uncircumcised Philistine that he should defy the armies of the living God?" (1 Sam. 17:26, *NIV*). "David said to Saul, 'Let no one lose heart on account of this Philistine; your servant will go and fight him. Your servant has killed both the lion and the bear; this uncircumcised Philistine will be like one of them, because he has defied the armies of the living God. The LORD who delivered me from the paw of the lion and the paw of the bear will deliver me from the hand of this Philistine'" (vv. 32,36-37, *NIV*). Even more impressive is what David said to the giant:

> You come against me with sword and spear and javelin,
> but I come against you in the name of the LORD Almighty,

the God of the armies of Israel, whom you have defied. This day the LORD will hand you over to me, and I'll strike you down and cut off your head. Today I will give the carcasses of the Philistine army to the birds of the air and the beasts of the earth, and the whole world will know that there is a God in Israel. All those gathered here will know that it is not by sword or spear that the LORD saves; for the battle is the LORD's, and he will give all of you into our hands (vv. 45-47, *NIV*).

The Israelites felt helpless because they saw the giant in relationship to themselves, but David saw the giant in relationship to God. The spies also saw the giants in the land in relationship to themselves, except for Joshua and Caleb who saw through the eyes of faith. Joshua and Caleb knew that the battle was the Lord's. We must believe the same if we are ever going to experience any victory in this life. Jesus has pulled up the stakes. He has taken the glass partition away. The veil keeping us from the holy One has been removed. God is with us, and nothing is impossible for Him. We can be like Joshua and Caleb and believe that we are never helpless with God, or we can be like those who choose to believe that they are as helpless now as they were before Christ.

CHILDHOOD ROOTS

Most learned helplessness is the result of early childhood experiences. Lacking the presence of God in our lives and the knowledge of His ways, we learned how to survive, defend and protect ourselves. Many felt defeated from the beginning, because the messages they received from the world had often been negative: *You can't do that; you'd better let me do it. You're not big enough or smart enough. You'll never amount to anything. It's a dog-eat-dog world out there, so be careful and watch your backside.* With these messages it is no wonder why we start to believe that we can't.

It has been estimated that 95 percent of the world's population is pessimistic by nature. Even the weatherman says, "There will a 35 percent chance of rain tomorrow." They never say there will be a 65 percent chance of sunshine. News anchors don't report the good things that happen on any particular day; they only report the bad news, which cannot help but give the population a distortion of reality. Three news helicopters and 25 police officers will follow a fugitive in a car pursuit for hours, but nobody follows the good guys who set about their day encouraging others. There are also blessing snatchers everywhere: "I see you bought that brand of car. I bought one once and it was a lemon." Even in churches people are prone to point out the imminent dangers and the sad state of affairs in the world, rather than encourage one another to live above their circumstances with great confidence in God: "I heard that you have just become a Christian. Congratulations, now you have an enemy you never had before!"

When depressed people feel helpless, they generally feel lethargic, cautious, fatigued, tired and pessimistic. These symptoms make considering new ways to overcome old problems difficult. We mentioned earlier the research by Dr. Henn (see chapter 3) that concluded that just as neurochemistry affects behavior, changes in behavior affect neurochemistry. In such cases a physical intervention may be necessary in order to jump-start the recovery process. Such may be the case when Elijah fled from Jezebel.

PHYSICAL INTERVENTION

Elijah showed incredible confidence in God and was recognized by the king's men as the "Man of God" (2 Kings 1:9,11,13, *NIV*). Elijah witnessed the incredible power of God displayed against the prophets of Baal (see 1 Kings 18). But when the wicked Jezebel heard of it, she responded, "May the gods deal with me, be it ever so severely, if by this time tomorrow I do not make your life like that of one of them" (1 Kings 19:2, *NIV*). "Elijah was afraid and ran for his life. When he came to Beersheba in Judah,

> WE ARE MOST VULNERABLE
> WHEN OUR ENERGY IS SAPPED
> FROM VICTORIOUSLY FIGHTING
> THE GOOD FIGHT AND WE ARE
> BRIMMING WITH CONFIDENCE.

he left his servant there, while he himself went a day's journey into the desert" (vv. 3-4, *NIV*). He believed a lie! This great man of God actually believed a lie, as any one of us can! Then, in despair, "'I have had enough, LORD,' he said. 'Take my life; I am no better than my ancestors.' Then he lay down under the tree and fell asleep" (vv. 4-5, *NIV*).

Elijah exhibited all the classic signs of depression. He was afraid, fatigued and felt like a lonely, helpless failure, which can potentially happen to the best of us, especially after a mountaintop experience. We are most vulnerable when our energy is sapped from victoriously fighting the good fight and we are brimming with confidence. Our confidence in God can easily turn to self-confidence when we let our guard down: "So, if you think you are standing firm, be careful that you don't fall!" (1 Cor. 10:12, *NIV*).

Notice what God did. "All at once an angel touched him and said, 'Get up and eat.' He looked around, and there by his head was a cake of bread baked over hot coals, and a jar of water. He ate and drank and then lay down again" (1 Kings 19:5-6, *NIV*). God in His mercy prescribed some food and rest for His discouraged servant. When our electrolytes are depleted and our body is malfunctioning for lack of nutrition, we need to address these deficiencies through good nutrition, exercise and rest.

Nutrition and Dietary Supplements

Many health-food experts recommend supplementing your diet with amino acids for depression. The most common is DLPA (D,L-phenylalanine), which is available in capsules at health-food stores. It is nontoxic, but it may increase blood pressure. The experts usually suggest taking DLPA along with vitamin C, vitamin B6 and fruit or fruit juice about 45 minutes before breakfast. Taken on an empty stomach, DLPA is absorbed into the blood and brain. The body uses it to synthesize more of the neurotransmitters that increase wakefulness and energy. Another amino acid, L-tyrosine, has a similar effect on brain chemistry.

A common herbal treatment for depression is Saint-John's-wort. Researchers have shown that it can improve mood and the quality of sleep in depressed people. This natural herb can be bought over the counter, but we recommend that you consult a good nutritional doctor or health-food expert for proper dosage.

God created many fruits and vegetables that were intended to be cultivated and harvested for the preservation of human life. Saint-John's-wort was created by God. There are probably many other natural remedies waiting to be discovered. Because of the pressures of living in these last days, the proper balance of rest, exercise and diet is even more essential. Couple that with the fact that the soils that produce our grains are becoming more and more depleted of their mineral content, it may be more necessary than ever to supplement our diets with vitamins and minerals.

Another nutritional remedy that should be considered for depression is vitamin B12. A B12 deficiency is notorious for causing a variety of changes in the way our nervous system functions. A B12 deficiency can be corrected in some patients through a B12-rich diet or nutritional supplements, but often this will not be sufficient. That's because the deficiency is frequently caused by the person's inability to absorb the nutrients in their intestines. If this is the case, the vitamin needs a more direct route into the body through injections. Blood tests can verify B12 deficiencies. Many people with symptoms of depression have been helped by getting B12 injections.

Physical Fitness

After Elijah had eaten and rested, he was visited again: "The angel of the LORD came back a second time and touched him and said, 'Get up and eat, for the journey is too much for you.' So he got up and ate and drank. Strengthened by that food, he traveled forty days and forty nights until he reached Horeb, the mountain of God" (1 Kings 19:7-8, *NIV*).

This passage suggests the importance of physical exercise, another ingredient of good physical and mental health. We don't want to read anything into the story of Elijah beyond what Scripture warrants, but the Bible does suggest he was physically fit.

Research indicates that aerobic exercises may be one of the best antidepressants. Aerobic exercises do not have to be particularly strenuous, but a certain energy level must be maintained for 20 to 30 minutes in order for them to be effective. Your pulse rate should double, your breathing should accelerate, and you should start perspiring. In addition to the well-known positive effect on the cardiovascular system, aerobic exercises increase the production of endorphins, which are the brain's own molecules associated with natural highs. Aerobic exercises are most effective when combined with good nutrition.

Rest and Recovery

Another important health consideration was implied when the angel said to Elijah that the journey was too much for him. Many people suffer from postadrenaline depression. We explained in chapter 3 that we get an adrenaline rush in response to demanding external circumstances. When these pressures become excessive, stress becomes distress and our systems break down. Our ability to physically cope is diminished. That is why there is usually an emotional low after an exhausting event. This kind of reactionary depression is common for people who have experienced a demanding week of work. Sundays can be depressing. We often feel this after a long conference, which is one long adrenaline rush.

Traveling 40 days and 40 nights on foot is not exactly observing the Sabbath. We all need to recognize the need for rest and recovery. It would be helpful to take an extra dosage of B-complex vitamins when facing a demanding schedule.

Whole Person

Good mental health cannot be totally separated from our physical health, which must be maintained with good nutrition, exercise and rest. Many people who struggle with depression are not physically healthy. Depression and physical health affect each other, and which came first cannot always be established. Do people's poor health contribute to their depression, or did their depressive state contribute to their poor health? We do not have to determine which came first in order to help those suffering, because the proper prescription relates to the whole person.

We are not suggesting that the angel did anything more than prescribe good nutrition and rest enabling Elijah to run for 40 days and nights. Scripture clearly shows that Elijah's problem began when he believed a lie. Nevertheless, God dealt with him as a whole person.

OBJECT LESSON

God wasn't finished with Elijah. Elijah's sense of helplessness needed to be corrected, so God gave Elijah an object lesson about His divine nature and what He required of Elijah:

> There he went into a cave and spent the night. And the word of the LORD came to him: "What are you doing here, Elijah?" He replied, "I have been very zealous for the LORD God Almighty. The Israelites have rejected your covenant, broken down your altars, and put your prophets to death with the sword. I am the only one left, and now they are trying to kill me too." The LORD said, "Go out and stand on the mountain in the presence of the LORD, for the LORD is about to pass by." Then a great and powerful wind tore the mountains apart and shattered the rocks before the LORD, but the LORD was not in the wind. After the wind there was an earthquake, but the LORD was not in the earthquake. After the earthquake came a fire, but the LORD was not in the fire. And after the fire came a gentle whisper. When Elijah heard it, he pulled his cloak over his face and went out and stood at the mouth of the cave. Then a voice said to him, "What are you doing here, Elijah?" (1 Kings 19:9-13, *NIV*).

God asked Elijah the same question again, and again Elijah defended his motives and actions. He didn't get the message. The truth is, God didn't send him there, and Elijah wasn't the only one left. There were 7,000 others who had not bowed their knees to Baal (see v. 18). God was not asking Elijah to bring in His kingdom program or bring judgment upon those who did not keep His Covenant. He was asking Elijah (and us) to trust Him and follow

Him wherever He led. He would bring judgment in due time and establish His kingdom His way and in His timing. That is not for us to decide, nor for us to accomplish. Our response to God is to trust and obey. Our perceived service for God may be the greatest enemy of our devotion to Him. We must resist the temptation to do God's work for Him. We are not instructed to petition God to bring judgment upon the disobedient in the form of winds, earthquakes and fires. If anything we are called to pray for mercy that God would withhold His judgment: "I looked for a man among them who would build up the wall and stand before me in the gap on behalf of the land so I would not have to destroy it, but I found none" (Ezek. 22:30, *NIV*).

Finally, God instructs Elijah to "Go back the way you came" (1 Kings 19:15, *NIV*). In other words, get back on track and don't isolate yourself from other people. Elijah found himself alone in the desert because he believed the enemy's lies. Although he was very zealous for God's work, he assumed sole responsibility for doing it himself. This is often referred to as the Elijah complex: *I alone am left, and I must vindicate the Word and reputation of God.* If you want to feel helpless, try doing God's work for Him.

How should we respond when the government ignores the prophetic voice of the Church, or when other people show contempt to the Lord? Is it our job to take on the government or try changing those who are blasphemous? Those who try will only become angry controllers or very depressed. We are called by God to submit to governing authorities and pray for them (see Rom. 13:1-6; 1 Tim. 2:1-2). We are to accept one another as Christ has accepted us (see Rom. 15:7). Yet that does not mean that we approve of sin or allow sin to determine who we are. Every Christian must learn how to establish scriptural boundaries to protect him- or herself from further abuse.[2]

The story of Elijah reminds us of a parable passed via the Internet. There was a man asleep in his cabin when he suddenly awoke. The Savior appeared in his room and it was filled with light. The Lord said, "I have work for you to do." He showed him a large rock and told him to push against that rock with all his might. This the man did, and for many days he toiled from sunup to sundown, his shoulder set squarely against the cold, massive surface of the rock, pushing with all his might. Each night the man returned to his cabin sore and worn out, wondering if his whole day had been spent in vain.

Seeing that the man showed signs of discouragement, Satan decided to enter the picture, placing thoughts in the man's mind such as, *Why are you doing this? You're never going to move it. You've been at it a long time and you haven't even scratched the surface.* The man began to sense that the task was impossible and that he was an unworthy servant because he wasn't able to move the massive stone.

These thoughts discouraged and disheartened him, and he started to ease up on his efforts. *Why am I doing this?* he thought. *I'll just put in my time, expending a minimum amount of effort, and that will be good enough.* And that he did, or at least planned on doing, until one day he decided to take his troubles to the Lord. "Lord," he said, "I have labored hard and long in your service, putting forth all my strength to do that which you have asked me. Yet, after all this time, I have not even nudged that rock a millimeter. What is wrong? Am I failing you?"

"My son," the Lord replied, "when long ago I asked you to serve me and you accepted, I told you to push against the rock with all your strength. That you have done. But never once did I mention that I expected you to move it, at least not by yourself! Your task was to push! Now you come to me all discouraged, thinking that you have failed, and you are ready to quit. But is that really so? Look at yourself. Your arms are strong and muscled, your back is sinewy and brown. Your hands are calloused and your legs have become massive and hard. Through opposition you have grown much, and your ability now far surpasses that which you used to have. Yet, still, you haven't succeeded in moving the rock. You come to me now with a heavy heart and your strength spent. I, my son, will move the rock. Your calling was to be obedient and to push, to exercise your faith and to trust in my wisdom. This you have done."

SANCTIFYING PROCESS

If we can do all things through Christ who strengthens us, then what are those "all things?" (see Phil 4:13). In other words, what is God's will for our lives? Paul clearly shares what God's will is for us: "It is God's will that you should be sanctified" (1 Thess. 4:3, *NIV*). In other words, we are to conform to the image of God, which we can do by His grace. We don't have any power to change ourselves—that also comes from Him. Allowing ourselves to be influenced by the world, the flesh and the devil will interrupt the sanctifying process. We also will curb the sanctifying process if trying to change the world becomes our primary focus. On the other hand, if our goal is to become the person God created us to be, no other person nor anything on planet Earth can prevent that from happening. The only one who can keep us from being that person is ourselves. Not even Satan can stop us.

Paul wrote, "And we rejoice in the hope of the glory of God. Not only so, but we also rejoice in our sufferings, because we know that suffering produces perseverance; perseverance, character; and character, hope. And hope does not disappoint us, because God has poured out his love into our hearts by the Holy Spirit, whom He has given us. You see, at just the right time, when we were still powerless, Christ died for the ungodly" (Rom. 5:2-6, *NIV*). Jesus defeated the devil and made us brand-new creations in Christ. He set us free from our past. We must destroy our mental strongholds that say, "I can't," and replace them with the truth that we can in Christ.

The human tendency is to think, *This marriage is hopeless*, and then believe the solution is to change spouses or try to change the spouse. The same holds true for any depressing situation. The answer is not to try to change what we can't or to let the situation determine who we are. Instead, the answer is to work with God in the process of changing ourselves. According to Paul, our hope does not lie in avoiding the trials and tribulations of life, because they are inevitable. Our hope lies in persevering through those trials and becoming more like Christ. The hope that comes from proven character will never disappoint us. It is only through proven character that we will positively influence the world.

Imagine the terrible emotional pain when a spouse leaves or when a child runs away. Anybody would be disappointed, discouraged and perhaps depressed by these difficult circumstances. They may likely think, *How can I win back the one I lost?* The unspoken underlying question all too often is, *How can I control my spouse or child or arrange the circumstances so that I can manipulate him or her into coming back?* That kind of control or manipulation is probably the reason they left in the first place. The fruit of the Spirit is not spouse control or child control, nor does God ensure us that external circumstances will always accommodate our desires. The fruit of the Spirit is self-control.

If you are going through a difficult situation, instead of trying to control or manipulate, a better question to ask yourself is, *If I haven't committed myself to be the spouse or parent or child that God has called me to be, will I now?* That is the only thing within your power to change, and it is by far the best thing you can do to win the other person back. However, even if you don't win the person back, you can come through the crisis with proven character.

Trials and tribulations are what God uses to refine your character and conform you to His image. The hope that comes from proven character will never disappoint. If your hope lies only in favorable circumstances or in trying to alter something that you have no right or ability to change or control, then you are going to suffer a lot of disappointed living in this fallen world. The following unknown poet said it well:

> "Disappointment—His appointment," change one letter, then I see
> That the thwarting of my purpose is God's better choice for me.
> His appointment must be blessing, tho' it may come in disguise,
> For the end from the beginning open to His wisdom lies.
>
> "Disappointment—His appointment," no good will He withhold,
> From denials oft we gather treasures of His love untold.
> Well He knows each broken purpose leads to fuller, deeper trust,
> And the end of all His dealings proves our God is wise and just.
>
> "Disappointment—His appointment," Lord, I take it, then, as such,
> Like clay in hands of a potter, yielding wholly to Thy touch.
> My life's plan is Thy molding; not one single choice be mine;
> Let me answer unrepining—"Father, not my will, but Thine."[3]

God never promises to take the person out of the slum, but He does promise to take the slum out of the person. He may even call some of us to go to the slum for the sake of ministry. It is the eternal plan of God to "provide for those who grieve in Zion—to bestow on them a crown of beauty instead of ashes, the oil of gladness instead of mourning, and a garment of praise instead of a spirit of despair. They will be called oaks of righteousness, a planting of the LORD for the display of his splendor" (Isa. 61:3, *NIV*). God promises to carry us through the trials and tribulations of life. Someone once said that success comes in *cans* and failure in *cannots*. Here are 20 cans of success that would do you well to memorize:

TWENTY CANS OF SUCCESS

1. Why should I say I can't when the Bible says I can do all things through Christ who gives me strength (see Phil. 4:13)?
2. Why should I worry about my needs when I know that God will take care of all my needs according to His riches in glory in Christ Jesus (see Phil. 4:19)?
3. Why should I fear when the Bible says God has not given me a spirit of fear, but of power, love and a sound mind (see 2 Tim. 1:7)?
4. Why should I lack faith to live for Christ when God has given me a measure of faith (see Rom. 12:3)?
5. Why should I be weak when the Bible says that the Lord is the strength of my life, and that I will display strength and take action because I know God (see Ps. 27:1; Dan. 11:32)?
6. Why should I allow Satan control over my life when God who is in me is far greater than he that is in the world (see 1 John 4:4)?

7. Why should I accept defeat when the Bible says that God always leads me in victory (see 2 Cor. 2:14)?

8. Why should I lack wisdom when I know that Christ became wisdom for me from God; and God gives wisdom to me generously when I ask Him for it (see 1 Cor. 1:30; Jas. 1:5)?

9. Why should I be depressed when I can have hope by remembering God's lovingkindness, compassion and faithfulness (see Lam. 3:21-23)?

10. Why should I worry and be upset when I can cast all my anxieties on Christ who cares for me (see 1 Pet. 5:7)?

11. Why should I ever be in bondage knowing that there is freedom where the Spirit of the Lord is (see Gal. 5:1)?

12. Why should I feel condemned when the Bible says there is no condemnation for those who are in Christ Jesus (see Rom. 8:1)?

13. Why should I feel alone when Jesus said He is with me always and He will never leave me nor forsake me (see Matt. 28:20; Heb. 13:5)?

14. Why should I feel like I'm cursed or have bad luck when the Bible says that Christ rescued me from the curse of the Law that I might receive His Spirit by faith (see Gal. 3:13-14)?

15. Why should I be unhappy when I, like Paul, can learn to be content whatever the circumstances (see Phil. 4:11)?

16. Why should I feel worthless when Christ became sin for me so that I might become the righteousness of God (see 2 Cor. 5:21)?

17. Why should I feel helpless in the presence of others when I know that if God is for me, who can be against me (see Rom. 8:31)?

18. Why should I be confused when God is the author of peace and He gives me knowledge through His spirit who lives in me (see 1 Cor. 2:12; 14:33)?

19. Why should I feel like a failure when I am more than a conqueror through Christ who loves me (see Rom. 8:37)?

20. Why should I let the pressures of life bother me when I can take courage knowing that Jesus has overcome the world and its problems (see John 16:33)?[4]

DEALING
WITH LOSS

*As I looked, the poplar rose in the shining air like a slender throat, and
there was an exaltation of flowers, the surf of apple tree delicately foaming.
All winter, the trees had been silent soldiers, a vigil of woods, their hidden
feelings scrawled and became scores of black vines, barbed wire
sharp against the ice-white sky.
Who could believe then in the green, glittering vividness of full-leafed summer?
Who will be able to believe, when winter again begins after the autumn burns
down again, and the day is ashen, and all returns to winter and winter's ashes,
Wet, white, ice, wooden, dulled and dreary, brittle or frozen.
Who will believe or feel in mind and heart the reality of the spring and of birth,
In the green warm opulence of summer, and the inexhaustible
vitality and immortality of the earth?*

DALMORE SCHWARTZ, "THE DECEPTIVE PRESENT"

The apostle Paul was the rising star in Jewish circles, but that changed when God struck him with blindness on the Damascus road. This sudden encounter with Jesus changed his life forever. He lost all his old friends, his social status and the bright future he had among the Jewish elite. History revealed that he went away for three years. It is only speculation, but chances are he went through a period of grief and depression. Experiencing loss is the primary cause of depression. The crisis itself does not cause the depression, but our mental perception of external events based on what we believe and how our mind has been programmed is what determines how we feel and how we react to any crisis or loss. During his three-year hiatus, Paul's mind was being renewed as he was overcoming his losses. Diagram 7.1 depicts the predictable cycle that everyone goes through when he or she experiences some crisis or loss in his or her life:

Diagram 7.1

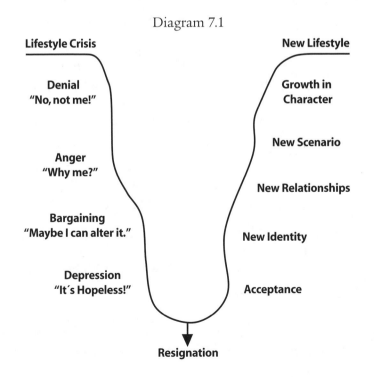

People have an established lifestyle that they assume will continue in the foreseeable future and hopefully improve. They make plans for the weekend and summer vacations assuming that life will go on as scheduled. Daily events are planned with the hope that they will still be alive, that their health will be okay and that all the necessary conditions will be favorable for life's going on as it presently is. During the summer of our soul, when everything is going well, we don't like to think that the days ahead will be any different. During the winter of our soul, it is hard to imagine that summer will ever come again.

Some people don't even consider any future consequences and say, "Let us eat and drink, for tomorrow we die" (1 Cor. 15:32). The Bible refers to such people as deceived and foolish. Paul's advice to them is, "Do not be misled: 'Bad company corrupts good character.' Come back to your senses as you ought, and stop sinning; for there are some who are ignorant of God—I say this to your shame" (vv. 33-34, *NIV*). Such people make no realistic plans, and consequently, they end up with no meaningful future. Others, even Christians, presume upon the future. James has some sobering advice for those who do:

> Now listen, you who say, "Today or tomorrow we will go to this or that city, spend a year there, carry on business and make money." Why, you do not even know what will happen tomorrow. What is your life? You are a mist that appears for a little while and then vanishes. Instead, you ought to say, "If it is the Lord's will, we will live and do this or that." As it is, you boast and brag. All such boasting is evil. Anyone, then, who knows the good he ought to do and doesn't do it, sins" (4:13-17, *NIV*).

The good, which we ought to do, is the Lord's will. Therefore, we must choose to live responsibly and one day at a time, believing that the will of God will not take us where the grace of God cannot keep us. In the Sermon on the Mount, Jesus tells us not to worry about tomorrow. And if God takes care of the lilies of the fields and the birds of the air, will He not much more provide for

> # THE WILL OF GOD WILL NOT TAKE US WHERE THE GRACE OF GOD CANNOT KEEP US.

us (see Matt. 6:28-31)? "Your heavenly Father knows that you need all these things. But seek first His kingdom and His righteousness, and all these things will be added to you. So do not worry about tomorrow; for tomorrow will care for itself. Each day has enough trouble of its own" (vv. 32-34).

That does not mean that we shouldn't make plans for the future. We must live responsibly and plan in order to live meaningful lives. The primary purpose for setting goals and making future plans is to give us purposeful direction for our lives today. Since we don't have control over many circumstances that can disrupt those plans, we need to say, "Lord willing, tomorrow we will do whatever; and regardless of what tomorrow holds, we will trust Him." This requires us to mentally and emotionally prepare for impermanence.

IMPERMANENCE

Nothing will be as it is five years from now. There is no permanence; there is only change. Tennessee Williams said, "We are all terrorized by the idea of impermanence."[1] Three times the Lord tried to prepare His disciples for this reality. In Mark 8 He said,

"That the Son of Man must suffer many things and be rejected by the elders and the chief priests and the scribes, and be killed, and after three days rise again. And He was stating the matter plainly" (vv. 31-32). The disciples' first response was denial. Peter actually rebuked the Lord (see v. 32). When He told them a second time, "they did not understand this statement, and they were afraid to ask Him" (9:32). The disciples didn't want to talk about it. Finally, the disciples were fearful as they approached Jerusalem when Jesus told them a third time (see 10:32-34). Jesus' purpose for telling them in advance was to prepare them for a major loss and give them hope. They would face persecution, and even though He would be killed, He would rise again.

To survive the crises of life, we must possess an eternal perspective, because time is a devouring beast for those who are outside of Christ. Without such a perspective, we cannot see the hope of summer during the emotional winters of our soul. The "deceptive present" masks the possibility of any hope for tomorrow. The psalmist's statement "Precious in the sight of the LORD is the death of His godly ones" (116:15) doesn't make sense from a time perspective. It only makes sense from an eternal perspective.

STAGES OF GRIEF

How do we respond to a crisis or loss in our lives? The crisis can be anything that interferes with well-intentioned plans. It could be the loss of a job, of health or of a spouse or loved one, or the end of one's dreams. Such losses sow the seeds of depression when we fail to see that our times are in His hands. The first response is denial—a refusal to accept the crisis or the loss. Some believe facing the truth is too painful. They consciously or subconsciously think, *This is all a bad dream or a trick that someone is playing on me. I refuse to even consider this as real.* Or they may consciously choose not to entertain thoughts that the crisis or loss actually happened:

I'll deal with this tomorrow or maybe next month. For others, it is too incredulous. They wonder, *How could this be happening to me? I'm a good person.* They may attempt to recover what is lost or go on living as though the crisis or loss never happened.

A depressed graduate student of mine was laid off from his engineering job. He couldn't face the shame of telling his spouse, even though the loss of his job resulted from his company's downsizing, not from his incompetence. Drenched in denial, he got dressed the next Monday morning and went to work as he normally did. By Wednesday his former employer had to call the police. Denial can last for 30 seconds or 30 years. When people finally face the truth, they usually feel angry or resentful because what happened to them wasn't fair. They think, *Why is this happening to me?* Their anger can be directed toward others, including God, who they think caused the crisis. Those who feel guilty or ashamed often direct their anger toward themselves.

Another stage is bargaining. People reason, *Maybe I can alter the situation or undo the events that led up to this crisis.* They become depressed when they discover they can't do anything to change what happened or to reverse the consequences. They believe the situation is hopeless and they are helpless to do anything about it. They try to undo it but cannot. Now they're not sure if they can go on living with the present circumstances. The tragic loss seems too much to bear. It is the winter of their souls. How can they imagine what summer is like, or if it is even going to come?

EXPLANATORY STYLES

Difficult times befall all of us on the road to wholeness and maturity. We learn how to accept and grow through childhood mistakes, adolescent embarrassments, young-adult misunderstandings and adult problems of all types. Some have had more than their share of afflictions.

Some individuals recover faster than others when faced with the same crisis. They may be physically healthier and have a greater network of support, but the primary determinant is their spiritual maturity. Our ability to recover is found in the way we perceive events that befall us. Our beliefs about life circumstances, ourselves and God determine if we respond in despair or in faith.

We interpret trials and tribulations through the grid of our previous learning experiences. We attempt to explain what happened and why it happened. How we explain difficult circumstances and painful events is drawn from our beliefs about God, ourselves, others and the way we think life works. Research leading to the theory of explanatory styles was conducted by Martin Seligman, the same person who did the pioneering research on learned helplessness. He asked, "'How do you think about the cause of the misfortunes, small and large, that befall you?' Some people, the ones who give up easily, habitually say of their misfortunes, 'It's me; it's going to last forever; it's going to undermine everything I do.' Others, those who resist giving in to misfortune, say, 'It was just circumstances; it's going away quickly anyway, and besides, there's much more in life.'"[2]

According to Seligman, we have developed different explanatory styles to deal with crises. These explanatory styles determine how soon and even whether we will recover from our losses. These explanatory styles are made up of the following three mental constructs: permanence, pervasiveness and personalization.

PERMANENCE

It will last forever.

Our recovery speed is greatly affected by whether we think the consequences of the crisis will have a short-term or a long-term effect on us. If we think that our problems today will negatively affect us all our lives, we will become pessimistic. We will believe the situation is hopeless and consequently feel depressed. This thought pattern is so common that we are hardly aware of it. Suppose a husband thinks, *My wife is cranky; she must be in a bad mood.* This is a short-term problem, and it will have very little lasting effect upon the husband. He may decide to avoid confrontation until the mood passes. But if the husband thinks, *My wife is cranky; she is an irritable person,* this is a long-term problem, and his response may be

- "I'm going to ignore her." That is denial.
- "I'm going to control her." That is anger.
- "I'm going to appease her." That is bargaining.
- "I'm going to change her." That will be depressing!
- "I'm going to avoid her." That is resignation.
- "I'm going to love her and learn to live with her." That is acceptance.

When someone reaches the depression stage on the crisis cycle, he or she is at a major crossroad. The person can believe that his or her predicament is permanent and resign, or the person can see it as impermanent and come to a point of acceptance. *I can't change what happened, but by the grace of God, I can change myself. I can come through this crisis a better person.*

A young couple attending seminary tried every possible means to have children. Their disappointment with God was written all over their faces. They had all but given up hope of having children. They had one other option, but it was very expensive and an unnatural means of child reproduction. They had what is called reactionary depression. At first they were angry at God, and then they tried bargaining with Him. *Lord, will you let us have children if we promise to go to the mission field?* All they heard from heaven was silence. I suggested the possibility that

God didn't want them to have children of their own. "You mean just give up?" she said. "No, that would be resignation," I responded. "I think you should consider trusting God again and accepting His will for your life. There may be reasons that you shouldn't have children that we don't know. We only see one little piece of a giant puzzle, but God sees the whole picture. If God has laid it on your heart to have children, then maybe He wants you to consider adoption as an alternative."

There are many crisis events and losses that cannot be altered. We have to learn how to live with the consequences of living in a fallen world, such as losing a spouse to death or losing a leg in an accident. While the loss is permanent, it doesn't have to negatively affect us permanently. Such crises can make or break us, depending on how we respond. God does not intend the crises of life to destroy us, but crises do reveal who we are. They expose our character and reveal what we believe.

Difficult circumstances are opportunities to adjust our course of life. When a pilot encounters turbulent air, he or she may consider going higher or lower, but stopping is a poor option. Someone said that a bend in the road is not the end of the road unless you fail to make the turn.

Joni Eareckson Tada felt that her life had come to the end of the road when she was paralyzed after a swimming accident. In a June 1993 interview recorded on a Focus on the Family broadcast, she said, "I wanted to end my life, and the frustration I felt at not being able to do that only intensified my depression. I was so desperate, I begged one of my friends to help me end it all."[3] Thank God that she didn't end her life, and thank God that He enabled her to make the bend in the road and become a blessing to millions.

The Lord never sees our troubles as permanent. To Him they are momentary: "For our light and momentary troubles are achieving for us an eternal glory that far outweighs them all"

(2 Cor. 4:17, *NIV*). The Lord said to the troubled nation of Israel, "'For I know the plans I have for you,' declares the LORD, 'plans to prosper you and not to harm you, plans to give you hope and a future'" (Jer. 29:11, *NIV*). Even when the children of Israel failed Him badly, God showed mercy toward them and restored what was lost: "I will repay you for the years the locusts have eaten" (Joel 2:25, *NIV*). Whatever losses we suffer, God will make them right in the end.

When we are in the darkness of depression, it is easy to believe the lie that God's favor is only momentary and His anger will last forever. But the truth is, "his anger lasts only a moment, but his favor lasts a lifetime; weeping may remain for a night, but rejoicing comes in the morning" (Ps. 30:5, *NIV*). Winter is not permanent, even though you can't sense the warmth of summer. You must choose to believe that summer comes. When you think that your crisis is permanent, then consider again Jeremiah's words:

> I remember my affliction and my wandering, the bitterness and the gall. I well remember them, and my soul is downcast within me. Yet this I call to mind and therefore I have hope: Because of the LORD's great love we are not consumed, for his compassions never fail. They are new every morning; great is your faithfulness (Lam. 3:19-23, *NIV*).

PERVASIVENESS

It will ruin my whole life.

The concept of pervasiveness refers to the extent that a crisis can affect other areas of our lives. An example of pervasive thinking is to conclude that if I failed in one endeavor, then I must be a total failure, or to think that my life is over if I were turned down or rejected by someone on whom I based my whole future. Susan went through a painful breakup with her boyfriend. She mourned the loss of a loved one with whom she had hoped to spend the rest of her life. *Will anyone ever want to marry me?* she wondered. Susan cried incessantly for the first two and a half days and on and off again after that. She didn't want to be around anybody, and she began missing work. She thought, *My employer will probably fire me anyway, so why bother trying?* Her friends called, but she often didn't return their phone calls; and when she did, she was cold and distant. The loss she experienced in one area of her life was projected onto every other area. Consequently, she felt no hope.

> NEVER FORGET THAT WHAT YOU HAVE TO GAIN IN CHRIST IS FAR GREATER THAN ANY LOSS YOU WILL BE CALLED TO ENDURE.

Don't let one loss infiltrate other aspects of your life. If you experience one loss, you are not a loser. If you fail to accomplish one goal, you are not a failure. If you get laid off at work, it doesn't mean that you are an irresponsible dad, a bad husband or an incompetent Sunday School teacher. The tendency of this kind of thinking is to rest our sense of worth on one relation-ship, one experience, one idea or one plan. When plans or rela-tionships don't last or fail to materialize, don't wrongly deem yourself a failure.

A Time to Mourn

It is natural, normal and certainly not sinful to mourn the loss of anything that is morally good or even morally neutral. Concerning the loss of a loved one, Paul said, "Brothers, we do not want you to be ignorant about those who fall asleep, or to grieve like the rest of men, who have no hope. We believe that Jesus died and rose again" (1 Thess. 4:13-14, *NIV*). Our hope lies in the finished work of Christ, not in the things of this world that we have no right or ability to control. We grieve for that which we lose, because we have become attached to certain people, places, ideas and things. The extent of the grief is determined by the degree of attachment to that which we lost.

In Losing We Can Still Win

Paul was deeply attached to the Pharisaic traditions and customs of his people, and he had worked hard to achieve his status in life. For Paul to give it all up required a massive intervention by God, and it came suddenly on the Damascus road. All Paul's future plans were dashed in a moment. *Why, God? Why did you do this to me? Nobody has been more zealous for You than I.* To make matters worse, his only hope would come from the Church he so fervently persecuted. Reflecting on this later in life, he wrote:

> But whatever things were gain to me, those things I have counted as loss for the sake of Christ. More than that, I count all things to be loss in view of the surpassing value of knowing Christ Jesus my Lord, for whom I have suffered the loss of all things, and count them but rubbish so that I may gain Christ (Phil. 3:7-8).

Jim Elliot, the martyred missionary, wrote, "He is no fool who gives what he cannot keep to gain what he cannot lose."[4] Everything we presently possess we shall someday lose. Being willing to sacrifice the natural and temporal to gain the spiritual and eternal is the central teaching of all four Gospels:

> For whoever wishes to save his life will lose it; but whoever loses his life for My sake will find it. For what will it profit a man if he gains the whole world and forfeits his soul? (Matt. 16:25-26).

The first reference to life in the above verse, *psyche*, refers to the natural life. The second reference to life, *zoe*, refers to the spiritual life that comes from God. The people who find their identity, purpose and meaning in life in the natural order of this physical world will eventually lose them. Those who find their life in God will keep it for all eternity. Whatever name we make for ourselves, whatever fame we achieve, whatever earthly position we attain and whatever treasures we amass will all be left behind. Attachments to this world subtract from our attachment to Christ. Nothing can separate us from the love of God, and we will suffer no debilitating loss that we cannot endure if we find our life, identity, acceptance, security and significance in Christ.

Prolonged depression after a loss signifies an overattachment to people, places, ideas and things that we have no right or ability to control. People simply will not let go of something they are going to lose anyway or have already lost. In Africa, people catch monkeys by hollowing out coconut shells and attaching chains to the shells. The other ends of the chains are tied to trees or stakes in the ground. Then, monkey food is placed in the hollow shells. The monkeys put their fists into the shells to get the food. But when the monkeys make a fist around the food, they can no longer extract their hands from the shells. The people simply detach the chains from the trees or stakes and walk off with the monkeys. Why don't the monkeys just let go? Probably because of the same reason we don't.

PERSONALIZATION

It's me! It's all my fault!

The third mental construct is to take personal responsibility for something we didn't cause or couldn't control. In personalization, the depressed person feels responsible for another person's anger, the downsizing of a corporation, bad weather, not knowing the future and a host of other uncontrollable circumstances and situations. Children become depressed when their parents get divorced, because they think it is their fault. Perfectionists often struggle with depression, because they have a tendency to blame themselves for everything. One little crisis upsets their idealized world and they believe, *It's my fault.* Driven to achieve their self-made goals, they become overly sensitive to any failure or crisis.

Personalization distorts people's perception of reality. When a crisis erupts at work, some think, *What did I do now?* Some people obsessively review an incident looking for what they did wrong. Their thinking is dominated by "if only's." *If only I had done that she would never have left me. If only I had joined the Navy when I had a chance.* Their identity and sense of worth is wrongly determined by the outcome of life events.

Blaming ourselves for every crisis in life and for every imperfection will perpetuate failure identity and depression. Many people who personalize were wrongly accused in early childhood, so they have come to believe that they have a part to play in every negative thing that happens. Paul wrote, "Let no one keep defrauding you of your prize by delighting in self-abasement" (Col. 2:18). Others are just victims of the one who accuses them day and night. They never understood the spiritual battle for their minds, nor learned how to take every thought captive to the obedience of Christ.

On the other hand, blaming others is a sure way to become bitter, angry, proud, self-serving and abusive. Self-exaltation is as bad as self-condemnation: "For by the grace given me I say to every one of you: Do not think of yourself more highly than you ought, but rather think of yourself with sober judgment, in accordance with the measure of faith God has given you" (Rom. 12:3, *NIV*). It doesn't do any good to blame others, and it doesn't do any good to blame ourselves. Neither pride nor false humility are proper responses to the trials and tribulations of life.

FREEDOM

Now I'll never get the promotion I wanted (permanence). *I'm a total failure in life* (pervasiveness). *It's my fault that our company didn't get the contract* (personalization). The mental constructs of permanence, pervasiveness and personalization dominate the way depressed people think. If you experience loss in one area, don't generalize it into a total life crisis. Keep it specific. If you experience a crisis today, don't allow it to affect you tomorrow. Keep short accounts. If the world is disintegrating around you, don't accept the blame when it's not appropriate! If you suffer the consequences of a bad decision, then change what you can, minimize your losses and move on. If you commit a willful act of sin, then own up to it. "If we confess our sins, he is faithful and just and will forgive us our sins and purify us from all unrighteousness" (1 John 1:9, *NIV*).

Depression intertwines body, soul and spirit, which are all regulated by what we believe. Jesus said, "You will know the truth, and the truth will make you free" (John 8:32). Choosing to believe the truth and living by faith is the essential prerequisite for living an emotionally healthy and productive life. But the converse is also true. Believing a lie and thinking unwholesome thoughts fuels depression and leads to bondage. You can change what you believe and how you think, which must happen if you are going to be depression free.

CRISIS STEPS

From		**To**	
Permanent:	"Forever"	Temporary:	"For a season"
Pervasive:	"In everything"	Specific:	"In this one thing"
Personal:	"I'm the problem"	Impersonal:	"It's a problem"

Consider the story of a frog who hopped around a pasture. It rained the day before, and the soil was very damp. A truck drove through the pasture and cut deep ruts into the ground. Unintentionally, the frog bounced into one of those ruts and got stuck. He made a halfhearted attempt to hop out, but he didn't make it. The rut was too deep.

The next day a few of his friends came looking for him; they found him stuck in a rut. They encouraged him to try again, but he said it was hopeless. He was permanently stuck in a rut. *Now I'm no good for anything,* he thought. *It was probably my fault that it rained the other day. That was God's way of getting even with me for not being a better frog.* For five straight days the other frogs came by to encourage him, but he remained stuck in his rut. On the sixth day his friends were surprised to see him hopping around the field. They asked him how he managed to get unstuck. The frog said, "A big truck came along and I had to get out of there!"

How do we get unstuck? We don't do it by denying the crisis. The first step is to define the crisis or loss and put it into perspective. Analyzing the loss from an eternal perspective helps to determine if the perceived loss is real or only imagined. Many people go through all the crisis cycle steps (see diagram 7.1) only to find out that what they believed or heard wasn't true. This can easily happen in the early stages of physical illnesses. One lady was so sure that her husband was going to die from cancer that she was bargaining with God to save his life when she found out it wasn't cancer at all.

LOSS

It is possible to go through the stages of anger, bargaining and depression even when the crisis is only a potential loss that is feared. After Hal Baumchen and I wrote *Finding Hope Again*, a lawyer shared his story with me. He was working for a very prestigious law firm when the rumor started floating around that there was going to be a countersuit filed against him and the firm. He started worrying about it incessantly until the possibility became a fact in his mind. He was so emotionally distraught that he resigned his position and sought medical treatment. After taking medications for a year, he read our book. He realized that his loss was only imagined. Essentially he believed a lie, just like Elijah, and ran.

Every real loss will result in some degree of mourning. Denying the loss only robs us of the comfort we need. Jesus said, "Blessed are those who mourn, for they shall be comforted" (Matt. 5:4). Christians are real people who bleed when they are cut and cry when they are hurt. It takes time to adjust to the loss. However, excessive grief over loss can turn into depression, which may indicate that too much value was placed on the attachment. This requires an honest evaluation of the loss in light of eternity and a decision to let go of the past and grab hold of God as Paul exhorts us:

> Not that I have already obtained all this, or have already been made perfect, but I press on to take hold of that for

which Christ Jesus took hold of me. Brothers, I do not consider myself yet to have taken hold of it. But one thing I do: Forgetting what is behind and straining toward what is ahead, I press on toward the goal to win the prize for which God has called me heavenward in Christ Jesus. All of us who are mature should take such a view of things. And if on some point you think different-ly, that too God will make clear to you. Only let us live up to what we have already attained (Phil. 3:12-16, *NIV*).

Casting blame or feeling guilty are inappropriate responses to loss and will only prolong the grieving period. We must accept the cards that have been dealt to us, realizing that God "causes His sun to rise on the evil and the good, and sends rain on the righteous and the unrighteous" (Matt. 5:45). We are all in this boat together and none of us will make the journey without fac-ing trials and tribulations. Even if you were to live a perfect life, you would still experience considerable loss. Never forget that what you have to gain in Christ is far greater than any loss you will be called to endure. We don't bargain with God. We humbly submit to Him and pray the serenity prayer:

> *God, grant me the serenity*
> *to accept the things I cannot change,*
> *the courage to change the things I can*
> *and the wisdom to know the difference.*[5]

Crisis recovery precipitates a deeper evaluation of who we really are. We may realize that we have placed too much of our identity in the things we do and not enough in who we are in Christ. The wife who finds her identity in marriage will experi-ence far greater loss when her husband leaves her than the woman who deeply understands what it means to be a child of

God. The man who finds his identity in his job will suffer great loss when he loses it. We received this letter from a pastor:

> I have been reading your two books *Victory over the Darkness* and *The Bondage Breaker*. I wanted to thank you for giving me two tools that I really needed. I'm the founding pastor of this church having begun 15 years ago. I am in the first steps of recovering from a church split. I have never known pain like this before, but I am finding it to be a tremendous time of learning and growth in the Lord. Your *Victory over the Darkness* book has been especially helpful in that I have tried to find too much of my identity in what I do as a pastor and not enough in who I am as a saint.

Such crises not only help us clarify who we are and why we are here, but they also precipitate the need for new relationships and the need to construct new scenarios for our lives. These changes are necessary for our growth in the Lord, but we will never make those changes unless we are forced to do so. Buzz Aldrin, the second man to walk on the moon, said, "My depression forced me at the age of forty-one to stop and, for the first time, examine my life."[6] We can easily get stuck in the same old ruts until God brings a truck along and we have to move. It is just God's way of disciplining us for our own good, according to Hebrews 12:7-11 (*NIV*):

> Endure hardship as discipline; God is treating you as sons. For what son is not disciplined by his father? If you are not disciplined (and everyone undergoes discipline), then you are illegitimate children and not true sons. Moreover, we have all had human fathers who disciplined us and we respected them for it. How much more should we submit to the Father of our spirits and live!

Our fathers disciplined us for a little while as they thought best; but God disciplines us for our good, that we may share in his holiness. No discipline seems pleasant at the time, but painful. Later on, however, it produces a harvest of righteousness and peace for those who have been trained by it.

God wants us to share in His holiness. The purpose of His discipline is to produce godly character. Remember, we all will be victimized as the inevitable consequence of living in a fallen world. Whether we remain a victim is our choice. We have the potential to come through every crisis a better person than we were before. The resultant lifestyle will be higher and more godly. Therefore, in the winter of your discouragement, lift up your eyes to heaven and recall in your mind that your hope is in God, and you will again experience the warmth of summer and the harvest of fall.

SURVIVING
THE CRISIS

I think we've lost the knowledge that happiness is overrated, that in a way, life is overrated. We've lost somehow, a sense of mystery about us, about our purpose, our meaning and our role. Our ancestors believed in two worlds and understood this world to be the solitary, poor, nasty, brutish and short one. We are the first generation of man that actually expected to find happiness here on Earth, and our search for it has caused such unhappiness. The reason? If you do not believe in another, higher world, if you believe in only the flat, material world around you, if you believe that this is your only chance for happiness, if that is what you believe, then you are not disappointed when the world does not give you a good measure of its riches—you are despairing.

PEGGY NOONAN, SPEECHWRITER FOR PRESIDENTS REAGAN
AND GEORGE H. W. BUSH

We live in a fallen world. Life on this planet isn't always easy or fair. We want things to go our way, but they often don't. We want justice to prevail, but that will not happen perfectly in this lifetime. God will make everything right in the end, but until then we will live with many injustices. We are tempted to think that Christians shouldn't have to suffer if they live a righteous life, but members of the Early Church suffered greatly at the hands of the religious establishment. After being beaten for sharing what they believed, "They went on their way from the presence of the Council, rejoicing that they had been considered worthy to suffer shame for His name" (Acts 5:41). "Indeed, all who desire to live godly in Christ Jesus will be persecuted" (2 Tim. 3:12). More Christians are martyred for their faith today than in any other period of Church history.

WHY DO WE SUFFER?

First, Christians will suffer for the sake of righteousness. We will share in the glory of Christ if we "share in his sufferings" (Rom. 8:17, *NIV*). "If we endure, we will also reign with Him" (2 Tim. 2:12). "For just as the sufferings of Christ flow over into our lives, so also through Christ our comfort overflows" (2 Cor. 1:5, *NIV*).

Second, suffering will come as the consequence of our own sin and as the chastisement from our heavenly Father. David felt the heavy hand of God in physical and mental suffering as a result of his sin (see Ps. 32:3-5). However, do not assume (as Job's friends did) that personal suffering is only the result of our own personal sin.

Third, suffering will come simply from our human frailty as part of living in a fallen world. Our "outer man is decaying . . . day by day" (2 Cor. 4:16). Despite our natural aversion to pain and suffering, Scripture tells us that suffering is reality and a necessity in the life of the believer. In the words of J. I. Packer,

"Suffering Christianly is an integral aspect of biblical holiness, and a regular part of business as usual for the believer."[1]

SUFFERING IS VALUABLE

Physical pain is a necessary warning signal as one physician wrote: "Pain is a sign that action should be taken; it implies that if action is not taken, the survival chances of the organism are going to decrease."[2] Even lack of proper bodily nourishment is felt as pain. Suffering may be God's way of trying to motivate us to change. C. S. Lewis wrote, "God whispers to us in our pleasures, speaks in our conscience, but shouts in our pain."[3]

> SMALL TRIALS OFTEN MAKE US BESIDE OURSELVES, BUT GREAT TRIALS BRING US AGAIN BACK TO OURSELVES.

Sometimes it takes great suffering to get our attention. Small trials often cause us to be beside ourselves, but great trials bring us again back to ourselves. The darkness of despair, "like Plato's cave, is the place where all men come to know themselves."[4]

SUFFERING BUILDS CHARACTER

Jesus was made perfect through suffering (see Heb. 2:10), and "He learned obedience from what he suffered" (Heb. 5:8, *NIV*). In the incarnation, Jesus who was fully God, became fully human. The development of His humanity from infant to adult gives us a model that we ought to follow. In these statements there is no suggestion of prior disobedience or sinful flaws in Christ. Rather, they suggest He grew from immaturity to maturity in His humanity. His experience of suffering makes Him a compassionate high priest who comes to the aid of suffering people (see Heb. 4:14-15). Godly love flows only from those who have died to self-centeredness and who now live for others. Putting to death the old self that wants its way inevitably involves pain. We do not easily die to self-rule. "To render back the will which we have so long claimed for our own, is in itself, wherever and however it is done, a grievous pain."[5]

SUFFERING TEACHES LOVE

Suffering strips away any pretense of our relationship with God. It weans us from all that is not God in order that we might learn to love Him for who He is, not for what He gives. Saint Augustine wrote, "God wants to give us something, but cannot, because our hands are full—there's nowhere for Him to put it."[6] Suffering empties our hands so that God can give us Himself—the true treasure of life. C. S. Lewis wrote, "Now God, who has made us, knows what we are and that our happiness lies in Him. Yet we will not seek it in Him as long as He leaves us any other resort where it can even plausibly be looked for. While what we call 'our own life' remains agreeable, we will not surrender it to Him. What then can God do in our interests but make 'our own life' less agreeable to us, and take away the plausible sources of false happiness?"[7]

SUFFERING HELPS UNDERSTANDING

We live in a world of moral conflict. Biblical history reveals a battle between good and evil that has brought much suffering. Even God shares in this suffering because of what sin has done to His creation: "In all their distress he too was distressed" (Isa. 63:9, *NIV*). The reality of evil and the true nature of God's love for us would not be known except through the experience of suffering: "The only way in which moral evil can enter into the consciousness of the morally good, is as suffering."[8] C. S. Lewis wrote, "A bad man, happy, is a man without the least inkling that his actions do not 'answer,' that they are not in accord with the laws of the universe."[9]

Your suffering may be the opportunity to testify about God's sustaining grace to both believers and unbelievers. Doctors and nurses are far more impressed with godly patients who hold up well under suffering and face death without fear than with begging, pleading Christians who have no sense of their immortality.

No matter what the source of our suffering—whether directly from God's discipline, from the hand of another person or simply from the natural evil that is part of the fallen world—it is under God's control. In His infinite wisdom and love He allows suffering to come our way for His ultimate glory, for our growth in character and for our witness in this world. The question that Peter Kreeft raises is valuable to keep in mind as we experience suffering:

> Perhaps we suffer so inordinately, because God loves us so inordinately and is taming us. Perhaps the reason why we are sharing in a suffering we do not understand is because we are the objects of a love we do not understand . . . perhaps we are even becoming more real by sharing in sufferings that are the sufferings of God, both on earth, as part of Christ's work of salvation, and in heaven, as part of the eternal life of the Trinity, which is the ecstatic death to self that is the essence of both suffering and joy.[10]

SUFFERING HAS LIMITS

A comprehensive explanation for all of our sufferings may never be fully known to us in this lifetime. However, be assured that God always has a limit on the suffering that He allows for each of us. As God clearly set limits on the suffering that Satan could bring on Job, so He does for each of us. Some people obviously have broader shoulders upon which He places great burdens, allowing them to suffer for righteousness' sake, such as Job and Paul. Suffering always comes with a temptation to respond with the sin of unbelief—either in a despondency that says, *God has forsaken me and there is no hope,* or in anger and rebellion. Satan scores another victory when victims respond with unbelief and walk away from their only source of hope.

SUFFERING POSSESSES HOPE

The promise of Scripture is not that God will keep us from suffering or even remove it quickly. Rather, He promises to provide grace to faithfully endure it. The psalmist does not say, "Cast your cares on the Lord and be carefree," but rather, "Cast your cares on the LORD and he *will sustain you*" (55:22, *NIV*, emphasis added). Similarly, we are not told that the causes of our anxieties will be removed but, rather, that in their midst we can experience the peace of God (see Phil. 4:6-7).

God's strength and comfort are present in our sufferings. He is the Father of compassion and the God of all comfort who comforts us in all our troubles (see 2 Cor. 1:3-4). The Greek word for "comfort" may also be translated as "encouragement." It is used here in its basic sense of "standing beside a person to encourage him when he is undergoing severe testing."[11] The present tense of the verb tells us that our God comforts us at *all* times—constantly and unfailingly in *all* of our sufferings.

It is suffering itself that helps to engender this perspective of hope that is so critical for overcoming depression. We can accept the sufferings that come our way if we understand the purpose and if we possess the hope that God will make things right in the end.

SUFFERING DEVELOPS TRUST

Life is wonderful when we sense God's presence, live victoriously over sin and know the truth that sets us free. Thank God for the mountaintop experiences when the circumstances of life are favorable. But are they always? What if you couldn't sense His presence for a season and God suspended His conscious blessings? What would you do if you faithfully followed God, and then one day all external circumstances turned sour like they did for Job? That has happened twice to us as a family. If it weren't for the message given in Isaiah 50:10-11, I'm not sure we would have survived the trials:

> Who is among you that fears the LORD, that obeys the voice of His servant, that walks in darkness and has no light? Let him trust in the name of the LORD and rely on his God. Behold, all you who kindle a fire, who encircle yourselves with firebrands, walk in the light of your fire and among the brands you have set ablaze. This you will have from My hand: You will lie down in torment.

Isaiah is talking about a believer, somebody who fears the Lord and obeys God yet walks in darkness. Isaiah is not talking about the darkness of sin, nor even the darkness of this world (i.e., the kingdom of darkness). He's talking about the darkness of uncertainty—a blanket of heaviness that hovers like a dark cloud over our very being—where the assurance of yesterday has been replaced by the uncertainties of tomorrow. God has suspended His conscious blessings. Attending church feels like a dismal experience. Friends seem more like a bother than a blessing. Could this happen to a true believer? What is the purpose for such a dark time? What is a person to do during these times?

Keep On Walking in the Light of Previous Revelation
First, Isaiah 50:11 tells us that we are to keep on walking. In the light we can see the next step—the path ahead is clear. We know a friend from an enemy, and we can see where the obstacles are. The Word has been a lamp unto our feet—it directed our steps— but now we begin to wonder if it's true. Darkness has overcome us. We are embarrassed by how feeling-oriented we are. Every natural instinct says *Drop out, sit down, stop!* However, the Word encourages us to keep on living by faith according to what we know to be true.

Joanne's and my first encounter with such a period of darkness came after Joanne discovered that she was developing cataracts in both eyes. In the late 1970s, doctors would not do lens implants for anybody under the age of 60. We had no alternative but to watch each of her eyes cloud over until she could barely see. Then her lenses were surgically removed. Thick cataract glasses were prescribed until she could be fitted with contact lenses. This was very traumatic for Joanne and took place over a two-year period.

Being a pastor's wife is pressure enough, but this additional trauma was more than she could handle. For Joanne's sake, I considered ways to serve the Lord other than being a senior pastor. I felt led to pursue my first doctoral degree, even though I had no idea what God had in store for us. Putting Joanne's welfare ahead of the ministry gave her some hope. Since our church was in the middle of a building program, we needed to stay until the project was complete. Within months after dedicating our new buildings, God released me from that pastorate. I was nearing the completion of my doctoral studies and facing the tasks of conducting research and writing a dissertation. I also wanted to finish a second seminary degree.

It was the most difficult educational year of my life. In one year, I completed 43 semester units, of which 17 were language studies in Greek and Hebrew. In the middle of that year I took my comprehensive exams, and by the end of the year I finished my research and doctoral dissertation. I also taught part-time at Talbot School of Theology.

We started that year with the assurance that $20,000 would be made available interest free. The plan was to pay off this loan when we sold our house. Not having to sell our house allowed us to keep our children in the same school for that year. After I completed my education, we were confident that God would have a place for us. For the next six months our life unfolded as planned, and then God turned out the lights.

We were sadly informed that the second half of the promised $20,000 wasn't going to come in. Having no other source of income, our cupboards were bare. I had no job and my educational goals were only half completed. I always considered myself a faithful man, but now I was on the brink of not being able to provide for the basic needs of my family. We were so certain of God's calling six months earlier, but now we were clouded in the darkness of uncertainty.

It all culminated two weeks before my comprehensive exams. Only 10 percent of the doctoral candidates had passed the previous testing that took place on two consecutive Saturdays, so there was a lot of pressure. If I didn't pass the exams, I couldn't start my research and dissertation. We had already invested three years of our lives and $15,000 in the program. Now we didn't even know where our next meal was coming from. We had equity in our house, but interest rates at the time were so high that houses simply weren't selling. The tension to create our own light was overwhelming. I looked into a couple of ministry opportunities, but we knew they weren't for us, and I couldn't accept them. The problem wasn't an unwillingness to work. I would have sold hot dogs to provide for my family. It wasn't a problem of pride either. We just wanted to know and to do God's will!

We began to wonder if we had made the wrong decision. God's leading was so clear the past summer. Why were we walking in darkness? It was as though God dropped us into a funnel, which got darker and darker. When we thought it couldn't get much darker, we hit the narrow part! Then at the darkest hour God dropped us out of the bottom of that funnel, and everything became clear.

It was about 2:00 A.M. on a Thursday when the dawn broke. Nothing changed circumstantially, but everything changed internally. I woke up with a great deal of excitement and a sense of joy. Joanne also woke up and she too could sense something had taken place. We had a conscious awareness of God in a remarkable way. No audible voices or visions, only God in His quiet and gentle way renewing our mind. My thought process went something like this: *Neil, do you walk by faith or do you walk by sight? Are you walking by faith now? You believed Me last summer, do you believe Me now? Neil, do you love Me, or do you love My blessings? Do you worship Me for who I am, or do you worship Me for the blessings I bring? What if I suspended My conscious presence in your life, would you still believe in Me?*

We knew then in a way what we had never known before. In my spirit I responded, *Lord, You know I love You, and of course I walk by faith, not by sight. Lord, I worship You because of who You are, and I know that You will never leave me nor forsake me. Forgive me, Lord, that I ever doubted Your place in my life or questioned Your ability to provide for all our needs.*

Those precious moments can't be planned or predicted. They're never repeatable. What we have previously learned from the Bible becomes incarnate during these times. Our worship is purified; our love is clarified. Faith moves from a textbook definition to a living reality. Trust is deepened when God puts us in a position where we have no other choice but to trust Him. We either trust or compromise our faith. The Bible gives us the only infallible rules of faith and knowledge of its object, but we learn to live by faith in the arena of life. This is especially true when circumstances are not working favorably for us. The Lord has a way of stretching us through a knothole, and just before we are about to break in half, suddenly we slip through to the other side. We will never go back to the same shape we were before.

The next day everything changed. The dean at Talbot School of Theology called to ask if I had taken another position. He asked me not to accept anything until we had the opportunity to talk. That Friday afternoon the dean offered me a faculty position, which I held for the next 10 years. That Friday evening a man from my previous ministry stopped by at 10:00 P.M. When we asked him what he was doing at our home at that hour of the night, he said that he wasn't sure. We invited him in thinking, *We'll figure out something.* Half jokingly we asked him if he'd like to buy our house, and he responded, "Maybe I would!" The next Tuesday he and his parents made an offer on our house that we accepted. Now we could sell our house because we knew where we were going to live.

Nothing changed externally before that morning, but everything changed internally. God can change in a moment what we could never change. We had previously made a commitment that helped sustain us during such times: *We will never make a major decision when we are down.* That alone has kept me from resigning after difficult board meetings or messages that bombed. The point is, Never doubt in darkness what God has clearly shown in the light. We are to keep on walking in the light of previous revelation. If it was true six months ago, it's still true. If we're serious about our walk with God, He will test us to determine whether we love Him or His blessings. He may cloud the future so that we can learn to walk by faith and not by sight or feelings.

Understand that God did not leave Joanne or me, He had only suspended His conscious presence so that our faith would not rest on our feelings, be established by unique experiences or be fostered by blessings. If our physical parents found themselves in difficult circumstances and couldn't afford any Christmas presents when we were young, would we have stopped loving them? Would we have stopped looking to them for direction and support? If God's "ministry of darkness" should envelop you, keep on walking in the light of previous revelation.

Don't Create Your Own Light

The second lesson we should learn from Isaiah is not to light our own fires. The natural tendency when we don't see it God's way is to do it our way. Notice the text again, "Behold, all you who kindle a fire, who encircle yourselves with firebrands, walk in the light of your fire" (50:11). God is not talking about the fire of judgment, He's talking about the fire that creates light. Notice what happens when people create their own light: "And among the brands you have set ablaze. This you will have from My hand: You will lie down in torment" (50:11). The Lord is saying, "Go ahead, do it your way. I will allow it, but misery will follow."

This is illustrated in the Bible. God called Abraham out of Ur into the Promised Land. In Genesis 12, God promised Abraham that his descendants would be more numerous than the sands of the sea or the stars in the sky. Abraham lived his life in the light of that promise, and then God turned out the lights. So many months and years passed that Abraham's wife, Sarah, could no longer bear a child by natural means. God's guidance had been crystal clear before, but now it looked like Abraham would have to assist God in its fulfillment. Who could blame Abraham for creating his own light? Sarah supplied the match by offering her handmaiden to Abraham. Out of that union came another nation, which has created so much conflict that the whole world lies down in torment. Jews and Arabs have not been able to dwell together peacefully to this day.

God superintended the birth of Moses and provided for his preservation. Raised in the home of Pharaoh, he rose to the second most prominent position in Egypt. But God had put into his heart a burden to set his people free. Impulsively, Moses pulled out his sword attempting to help God set His people free, and God turned out the lights. Abandoned to the back side of the desert, Moses spent 40 years tending his father-in-law's sheep. Then one day Moses turned to see a burning bush that wasn't consumed (see Exod. 3:1-2), and God turned the lights back on.

We're not suggesting that we may have to wait 40 years for the cloud to lift. In our life span that would be more time than an average person's faith could endure. But the darkness may last for weeks, months and, possibly for some exceptional people, even years. God is in charge and He knows exactly how small a knothole He can pull us through. "The One forming light and creating darkness, causing well-being and creating calamity; I am the LORD who does all these" (Isa. 45:7).

Now for Joanne's and my second period of darkness. Five years after Joanne's surgery to remove the lenses from both her eyes, her doctor suggested that she have a lens implant. So much progress had been made during those five years that implanting a lens was now considered outpatient surgery. At first Joanne was reluctant, and our insurance company wouldn't pay, calling the surgery cosmetic, but they finally came around. Joanne's doctor and I convinced her it was the best thing to do.

The surgery was successful, but Joanne emerged from the anesthesia in a phobic state. She had been anesthetized in surgery before, so I couldn't understand why she was so fearful now. I certainly could understand her apprehension before surgery, because having one's eyeball cut is not something one looks forward to. Just the thought of it can send shivers down one's spine. Her emotional state after surgery was somewhat troubled. Could the anesthetic itself have caused her emotional state? Could the nature of her postoperative care have been a factor? The cost for medical care has pushed many hospitals into day surgeries that leave no time for rest or recovery after such a treatment.

The nurses had to ask for my assistance in helping Joanne come out of the anesthetic. They wanted to clear a bed for other patients. Joanne was just one of several patients that day. Most people need more emotional care than that. If Joanne had been permitted to gradually recover from her experience and spend a night in the hospital, she may have recovered a lot better. Bringing Joanne home that afternoon was an ordeal for both of us. She just couldn't stabilize emotionally.

The possibility of this also being a spiritual battle became evident the next day. Joanne thought the foreign object in her eye had to come out. This made no sense at all since the surgery was successful. She could see with 20/30 vision. We didn't understand the battle for our mind then as we do today. Paul wrote, "I find then the principle that evil is present in me, the one who wants to do good" (Rom. 7:21). The evil that Joanne fought was not the physical kind; it was a lie of Satan that came at a very vulnerable moment.

It is painful to recall this, because much of what followed may have been avoided. Joanne's struggle with anxiety led to sleeplessness and finally depression. She went from her eye doctor to her primary-care doctor to her gynecologist to a psychiatrist. Since not one of them could find anything physically wrong with Joanne, each assumed she was a mental or hormonal case. They tried hormones, antidepressants and sleeping pills, but nothing seemed to work. She lost her appetite and her weight dropped significantly. She was hospitalized five times.

This Too Will Pass. Attempts at getting medical help became exceedingly expensive. Our insurance coverage ran out and we had to sell our house to pay the medical bills. Joanne couldn't function as a mother or wife. Our daughter, Heidi, wasn't sure if she could handle it if her mother died. Our son, Karl, withdrew into himself. I was caught in a role conflict. Was I Joanne's pastor, counselor or discipler, or was I supposed to be just her husband? I decided there was only one role I could fulfill in Joanne's life, which was to be her husband. If someone was going to fix Joanne, it would have to be someone other than me. My role was to hold Joanne every day and say, "This too will pass." We thought it would be a matter of weeks or months, but it turned into a 15-month-long ordeal. The funnel got narrower and narrower. Isaiah 21:11-12 had great meaning for us:

> One keeps calling to me from Seir, "Watchman, how far gone is the night? Watchman, how far gone is the night?" The watchman says, "Morning comes but also night."

A ministry of hope is based on the truth that morning comes. No matter how dark the night, morning comes. It's always the darkest before the dawn. During our darkest hour, when we weren't even sure if Joanne was going to live or die, morning came. Joanne had all but given up on any medical hope. A doctor in private practice was recommended to her. He immediately took Joanne off her medications and prescribed a much more balanced approach that dealt with depression and included good nutrition and B12 injections.

At the same time, there was a day of prayer at Biola University, where I taught. I had nothing to do with the program other than to set aside special time for prayer in my own classes. The undergraduate students had a Communion service that evening. Since I taught at the graduate level, I normally wouldn't go; but since work had detained me on campus that evening, I decided to participate. I sat on the gym floor with the undergraduate students and took Communion. It is unlikely that anybody was aware that it was one of the loneliest and darkest times of my life. I was committed to doing God's will and walking as best I could in the light of previous revelation. Nothing I did changed Joanne or the circumstances.

Morning Will Come. Joanne and I never once questioned God and we never felt bitter about our circumstances. The Lord had been preparing our heart and leading us into a ministry that helps believers resolve personal and spiritual conflicts. We sensed that the nature of our ministry was related to what we were going through, but we didn't know what to do about it. Should we abandon what we were doing to help others in order to spare our family? God was blessing my ministry in unprecedented ways, but we weren't being blessed. God stripped us of everything we owned. All we had left was each other and God. When there was nowhere else to turn, morning came!

If God has ever spoken to my heart, He did in that Communion service. There were no voices or visions. It was just the quiet, gentle way that He renews our mind. It didn't come by way of the pastor's message or the testimonies of the students, but it did come in the context of taking Communion. The essence of my thought process went like this: *Neil, there's a price to pay for freedom. It cost My Son His life. Are you willing to pay the price? Dear God, if that's the reason, I'm willing; but if it's some stupid thing I'm doing, then I don't want to be a part of it anymore.* I left the gym with the inward assurance that it was over. The circumstances hadn't changed, but in my heart I knew that morning had come.

Within a week, Joanne woke up one morning and said, "Neil, I slept last night." From that time on Joanne knew she was on the road to recovery. She never looked back and continued on to full and complete recovery. At the same time, our ministry took a quantum leap. What was the point of all this? Why did we have to go through such a trial?

Brokenness Is the Key to Ministry. First, we learned a lot about ourselves in those times of darkness. Whatever was left of our old natures that gave simplistic advice, such as, Why don't you read your Bible or work harder or pray more, was mercifully stripped away. Most people going through dark times want to do the right thing, but many can't or don't believe they can. We also had a better understanding of our limitations, and we deepened our roots in the eternal streams of life while severing ties with unlasting temporal things.

Second, we learned to be more compassionate. We learned to wait patiently with people, weep with those who weep and not instruct those who weep. We learned to respond to the emotional needs of people who have lost hope. Instruction will come later. I was a caring person before, but nothing like I am now, because of God's gracious way of ministering to me.

We had some "friends," like those who tried to help Job, who offered advice to us in our time of darkness, and we can tell you it hurt. What Job needed in his hour of darkness was a few good friends who would just sit with him. Job's friends did for one week, and then their patience ran out. We received meaningful help from the Church, especially those people who just stood by us and prayed. If God took away every external blessing and reduced our assets to nothing more than meaningful relationships, would those relationships be enough for us?

Most of the world has learned to be content with food and clothing, because they have no other choice. Paul said, "I know how to get along with humble means, and I also know how to live in prosperity; in any and every circumstance I have learned the secret of being filled and going hungry, both of having abundance and suffering need" (Phil. 4:12). This is an important lesson to learn. The final lot of Job was far better than it was at the beginning. Within two years of our losses, God replaced everything we lost, only this time it was far better, in terms of home, family and ministry. Be encouraged that God makes everything right in the end.

> BE ENCOURAGED THAT GOD MAKES EVERYTHING RIGHT IN THE END.

Third, I believe God brought Joanne and me to the end of our resources in order that we may discover His. In churches today there are not many sermons about brokenness. It's the great omission, and that's why the Great Commission can't be fulfilled. In all four Gospels, Jesus taught us to deny ourselves, pick up our cross daily and follow Him. When it was time for the Son of Man to be glorified, He said, "Truly, truly, I say to you, unless a grain of wheat falls into the earth and dies, it remains alone; but if it dies, it bears much fruit" (John 12:24). There is no painless way to die to ourselves, but it's necessary. It's the best possible thing that could ever happen to us: "For we who live are constantly being delivered over to death for Jesus' sake, so that the life of Jesus also may be manifested in our mortal flesh" (2 Cor. 4:11). If we are relying on degrees, diplomas, status and self-confidence, God is going to strip us of our self-sufficiency.

Moses was no good for God in Pharaoh's court until all earthly possessions and positions were stripped from him. Chuck Colson was no good for God in the White House, but he was good for God in prison. I had earned five degrees, but I wasn't much good for God until suffering had its perfect result. We can't set anybody free, but God can. Every book I have written and every tape I have recorded was all done after this period of brokenness. It was the birth of Freedom in Christ Ministries, which has spread all over the world. "No pain, no gain," says the bodybuilder. That is also true in the spiritual realm. Isaiah's second point is simply this: Don't create your own light. Man-made light is very, very deceptive.

Learn to Trust

The final point Isaiah makes is, "Let him trust in the name of the LORD and rely on his God" (50:10). Walking in darkness is a lesson in trust. Every great period of personal growth in Joanne's and my lives and in our ministry has been preceded by a major time of testing. One of the greatest signs of spiritual maturity is the ability to postpone rewards. The ultimate test would be to receive nothing in this lifetime and look forward to receiving our reward in the life to come. Listen to how the writer of Hebrews expressed it: "All these died in faith, without receiving the promises, but having seen them and having welcomed them from a distance, and having confessed that they were strangers and exiles on this earth. For those who say such things make it clear that they are seeking a country of their own" (11:13-14). Verses 39-40 read, "And all these, having gained approval through their faith, did not receive what was promised, because God had provided something better for us, so that apart from us they would not be made perfect."

God's will for your life is on the other side of a closed door, and you may never know what it is unless you resolve an issue on this side of the door. If God is God, He has the right to decide what is on the other side of the door. If you don't give Him that right and insist on doing your own thing, then you will play your own game and decide your own destiny on this side of the door. You will get your way, but you will miss your calling. "There is a way which seems right to a man, but its end is the way of death" (Prov. 14:12).

If Joanne and I had known beforehand what our family would have to go through to get to where we are today, we may not have come. But looking back, we can all say, "We're glad we came." God doesn't show us what's on the other side of the door for that reason. Remember, God makes everything right in the end, and it may not even be in this lifetime, as it wasn't for the heroes mentioned in Hebrews 11. Yet we believe with all our heart that when this physical life is over, all the faithful will be able to look back and say that the will of God is good, acceptable and perfect. I'm glad I came this way.

CHAPTER NINE

A COMMITMENT TO OVERCOME DEPRESSION

The apostle John records the story of a man who had been lame for 38 years. The Lord singled him out at the pool of Bethesda where many blind, lame and paralyzed people were gathered. Those present at the pool believed an angel would occasionally stir the waters and anybody who was in the pool at the time would be healed. But this poor man could never get to the pool before the waters stopped stirring. "When Jesus saw him lying there, and knew that he had already been a long time in that condition, He said to him, 'Do you wish to get well?'"(John 5:6).

That is either a cruel question or a very profound and penetrating one. Obviously it is the latter since the Lord asked it. "The sick man answered Him, 'Sir, I have no man to put me into the pool when the water is stirred up, but while I am coming, another steps down before me.' Jesus said to him, 'Get up, pick up your pallet and walk.' Immediately the man became well, and picked up his pallet and began to walk" (vv. 7-9). The context reveals that the man really didn't want to get well. He never asked Jesus to be healed, and he always had an excuse why others got to the pool and he couldn't. "Afterward Jesus found him in the temple and said to him, 'Behold, you have become well; do not sin anymore, so that nothing worse happens to you.' The man went away, and told the Jews that it was Jesus who had made him well" (vv. 14-15). This ungrateful man actually turned Jesus in to the religious authorities for healing him on the Sabbath!

THE KEY TO A CURE IS COMMITMENT

Do you want to get well? Are you willing to humble yourself and seek the help you need from God and others? Are you willing to face the truth and walk in the light? Do you want a partial answer or the whole solution? We must ask these tough questions for your sake. Over 50 percent of those struggling with depression never ask for help or seek treatment for their depression. There are adequate answers for depression, but you have to want to get well and be willing to do whatever it takes to be free. The key to any cure is commitment. We are not offering a quick fix or partial answer. If you follow the procedure in this chapter in the suggested order, you will have a comprehensive and adequate answer for your depression.

Recovery begins by saying, "I have a problem and I need help." Your diligence in reading to this point demonstrates your commitment to seeking the help you need to gain total victory. We have a God of all hope. He is "our refuge and strength, an ever-present help in trouble" (Ps. 46:1, *NIV*). The story of the lame man reveals that God is fully capable of healing people even against their will and regardless of their faith. Rest assured that your heavenly Father will be faithful to keep His Word and His Covenant: "Jesus Christ is the same yesterday and today and forever" (Heb. 13:8). Therefore, we offer the following steps to overcome depression.

1. SUBMIT TO GOD AND RESIST THE DEVIL

Matthew 6:33; James 4:7

If you desire to get well and if you are willing to assume responsibility for your own attitudes and actions, then we believe there is hope for you. E. Stanley Jones said, "I laid at Christ's feet a self of which I was ashamed, couldn't control, and couldn't live with; and to my glad astonishment He took that self, remade it, con-

> GOD CAN DO WONDERS WITH A BROKEN HEART IF YOU GIVE HIM ALL THE PIECES.

secrated it to kingdom purposes, and gave it back to me, a self I can now live with gladly and joyously and comfortably."[1]

We encourage you to trust God by submitting to Him and His ways, and by seeking a wholistic answer. He alone can bind up the brokenhearted and set the captive free. God can do wonders with a broken heart if you give Him all the pieces. In our Western world, we have been conditioned to seek every possible natural explanation and cure first. When that is not successful, *then there is nothing more that we can do but pray.* Scripture has a different order: "But seek first His kingdom and His righteousness, and all these things will be added to you" (Matt. 6:33). The first thing a Christian should do about anything is pray. We suggest the following prayer to begin the recovery process:

Dear heavenly Father, I come to You as Your child. I declare my total dependence on You and acknowledge that apart from Christ I can do nothing. Thank You for sending Jesus to die in my place in order that my sins could be forgiven. I praise You for Your resurrection power that raised Jesus from the grave in order that I too may have eternal life. I choose to believe the truth that the devil has been defeated and that I am now seated with Christ in the heavenlies. Therefore, I choose to believe that I have the power and the authority to do Your will and to be the person You created me to be. I submit my body to You as a living sacrifice and ask You to fill me with Your Holy Spirit. I desire nothing more than to know and do Your will, believing that it is good, perfect and acceptable for me. I invite the Spirit of truth to lead me into all truth that I may experience my freedom in Christ. I choose from this day forward to walk in the light and speak the truth in love. I acknowledge my pain to You, and I confess my sins, doubts and lack of trust. I now invite You to search my heart, try my ways and see if there is any hurtful way within me, and then You lead me into the everlasting way by the power and guidance of Your Holy Spirit. In Jesus' precious name I pray. Amen.

Seek an Intimate Relationship with God
A whole answer will require first and foremost the presence of

God in your life. Jesus is not an impersonal higher power. He is our Lord and our Savior who took upon Himself the form of a man and dwelt among us. He was tempted in every way and suffered a humiliating and agonizing death in order that we could have access to our heavenly Father. He invites us to come— "Come to me," Jesus said (Matt. 19:14; Mark 10:14, *NIV*). Jesus does not invite us to a physical church structure or program, He invites us into the very presence of God. We need His presence in our lives, because He is the source and strength of our lives. Another invitation is given to us in Hebrews: "Let us draw near to God with a sincere heart in full assurance of faith, having our hearts sprinkled to cleanse us from a guilty conscience and having our bodies washed with pure water. Let us hold unswervingly to the hope we profess, for he who promised is faithful" (10:22-23, *NIV*).

The greatest crisis that mankind ever suffered was when Adam and Eve lost their relationship with God. The only lasting answer is to reestablish an intimate relationship with God, who is our only hope. What Adam and Eve lost was life, and what Jesus came to give them and us was life. The moment we are born again, we possess that spiritual, or eternal, life, which is established by the blood of the Lord Jesus Christ and His resurrection. We maintain that relationship by living in harmony with our heavenly Father with a sincere heart. This may require resolving certain personal and spiritual conflicts between ourselves and God.

The Steps to Freedom in Christ helps you resolve any conflicts that may exist between you and your heavenly Father through repentance and faith in Him (see chapter 3). Essentially, the process helps you submit to God and resist the devil (see Jas. 4:7). Doing so eliminates the influence of the evil one and connects you with God in a personal and powerful way. You will then be able to experience the peace of God that guards your heart and your mind (see Phil. 4:7), and you will sense the Holy Spirit bearing witness with your spirit that you are a child of God (see Rom. 8:16). Now by the grace of God you will be able to process the remaining issues in this chapter.

Many people will be able to process the Steps by themselves, because Jesus Himself is the wonderful counselor. The chances of that happening are greatly increased if you first read my two books *Victory over the Darkness* (Regal Books, 2000) and *The Bondage Breaker* (Harvest House Publishers, 2000). We encourage you to get alone with God and give yourself three or four hours to go through the process. Find a quiet place where you will not be interrupted and where you can verbally go through the Steps.

You have nothing to lose by going through this process of submitting to God and resisting the devil, but you have a lot to gain. The Steps are nothing more than a fierce moral inventory intended to help you "clean house" and make room for Jesus to reign in His temple. In our experience, severe cases require the assistance of a godly encourager. If you really want to get well, you won't hesitate to ask a Christ-centered pastor or counselor for help.

Establish Yourself as a Child of God

Knowing who God is and who we are in Christ are the two most essential beliefs that enable us to live a victorious life. God loves us because God is love. It is His nature to love us. He couldn't do anything other than that. God is omnipotent; therefore, we can do all things through Christ who strengthens us (see Phil 4:13). God is omniscient; therefore, He knows the thoughts and intentions of our heart (see Heb. 4:12-13). He knows what we need, and He is able to meet that need. God is omnipresent; therefore, we are never alone. He will never leave us nor forsake us. We have become partakers of His divine nature, because our soul is in union with God (see 2 Pet. 1:4). That is what it means to be spiritually alive *in* Christ. He has defeated the devil, forgiven our sins, given us eternal life and made us His children if we have received Him into our life. "To all who received him, to those who believed in his name, he gave the right to become children of God" (John 1:12, *NIV*).

At the end of this chapter there is a page for you to use. On one side is a list of Scriptures affirming who you are in Christ, which shows how He meets your needs of acceptance, security and significance. On the other side is The Overcomer's Covenant in Christ, which is based on your position in Christ. When you feel discouraged and depressed, this will help you refocus your mind to the truth of who you are in Christ and the position you have in Him.

2. COMMIT YOUR BODY TO GOD AS A LIVING SACRIFICE

Romans 12:1

Depression is a multifaceted problem that affects the body, soul and spirit. Consequently, a comprehensive cure for depression requires a wholistic answer. There are many forms of biological depression, which can be detected by comprehensive blood tests and thorough medical examinations. However, a 10-minute HMO checkup will not be sufficient, nor will seeing a psychiatrist or doctor who *only* reads the symptoms in order to prescribe antidepressant medication. If your depression is primarily endogenous, you will want some corroborating evidence to validate the medical treatment. Find a medical doctor or psychiatrist who administers the appropriate tests, understands psychosomatic illnesses and understands the value of exercise, vitamins and mineral supplements.

There are many other forms of biological depression, which can be diagnosed and treated. A disorder of the endocrine system can produce depressive symptoms. The endocrine system includes the thyroid, parathyroid, thymus, pancreas and adrenal glands. The endocrine system produces hormones that are released directly into the blood system. The thyroid gland controls metabolism. An underactive thyroid (i.e., hypothyroidism) will cause changes in mood, including depression. The metabolism of sugar is especially important for maintaining physical and emotional stability. Hypoglycemia (i.e., low blood sugar) will likely be accompanied by emotional instability.

The pituitary gland in the brain produces ACTH, which stimulates the adrenal glands. The malfunctioning of either gland will produce lethargic behavior and depression. In chapter 3, we discussed the problem of adrenal exhaustion due to prolonged stress. Part of the recovery process includes sufficient rest and a diet supplemented with B-complex vitamins. It may be necessary for some people to get vitamin B12 injections. There are several causes for B12 deficiency, but the most common cause is aging. When we age, our stomachs produce less of the acid that is necessary to extract B12 from our food.

The fact that women suffer from depression more than men may be due to their biological nature: "The reproductive organs of the female are extremely prone to creating mood swings. The depression at the onset of menstruation, the premenstrual syndrome (PMS), the use of contraceptive pills, pregnancy, postpartum reactions, and menopause all revolve around the female's reproductive system. And as we currently understand it, the system is fraught with depression pitfalls."[2]

Many biological depression symptoms can be eliminated when you assume your responsibility to live a balanced life including rest, exercise and diet. To live a healthy life, you must be health oriented, not illness oriented. It is the same dynamic of winning the battle for your mind. The answer is not to renounce all the lies. The answer is to choose the truth. However, if you aren't aware that there are lies and if you ignore what your body is telling you, then you will likely fall victim to disease and the father of lies. Whenever you sense that you are slipping back into a depression, don't just succumb to it, take charge of your life by praying:

> *Dear heavenly Father, I submit myself to You as Your child,*
> *and I declare myself to be totally dependent on You. I yield my*
> *body to You as a living sacrifice, and I ask You to fill me with*
> *Your Holy Spirit. I renounce the lies of the evil one, and*
> *I choose to believe the truth as revealed in Your Word. I resist*
> *the devil and command all evil spirits to leave my presence.*
> *I now commit myself to You and my body to You as an instrument*
> *of righteousness. In Jesus' precious name I pray. Amen.*

3. BE TRANSFORMED BY THE RENEWING OF YOUR MIND
Romans 12:2

Depression can be divided into two categories. One is related to lifestyle and the other is precipitated by a crisis event. By lifestyle depression, we mean a depressive state that began in early childhood or has existed for many years. There is also some possibility that lifestyle depression has hereditary connections, which is more likely with bipolar rather than unipolar depression. In such cases, medication, along with godly counsel, may be required for complete recovery. It is far more common, however, that the cause for lifestyle depression can be traced to an oppressive upbringing or environment that created or communicated a sense of hopelessness and help-lessness.

Learned helplessness can be unlearned by the renewing of our mind. Over time our brains have been programmed to think negatively about ourselves, our circumstances and our futures. These negative thoughts and lies have been deeply ingrained. There have been thousands of mental rehearsals that have added to the feelings we are experiencing right now. The natural tendency is to ruminate on these negative thoughts. *New York Times* columnist Daniel Goleman explains in his book *Emotional Intelligence*, "One of the main determinants of whether a depressed mood will persist or lift is the degree to which people ruminate. Worrying about what's depressing us, it seems, makes the depression all the more intense and prolonged."[3]

How do you win the battle for your mind? Should you rebuke every negative thought? If you tried, that is all you would do for the rest of your life. You would be like a person stuck in the middle of a lake with a hammer in your hand trying to sub-merge 12 corks floating around your head. All your energy would be expended trying to keep the corks submerged while trying to tread water. Instead, you should ignore the corks and swim to shore. You overcome the father of lies by choosing the truth. You can do that if you have successfully submitted to God and resisted the devil.

There is a major difference between winning the spiritual battle for your mind and the long-term growth process of renewing your mind. It doesn't take long to establish your free-dom in Christ, but it will take you the rest of your life to renew your mind and conform to the image of God. There is no such thing as instant maturity, but the ability to experience your freedom in Christ can happen in a relatively short period of time. Once you have established your identity and freedom in Christ, the process of renewing your mind is quite easy. That is why we encourage you to go through *The Steps to Freedom in Christ* first.

Changing false beliefs and attitudes is necessary to overcome depression. The world will put you down and the devil will accuse you, but you don't have to believe either one. You have to take every thought captive to the obedience of Christ. In other words, you have to believe the truth as revealed in God's Word. You don't overcome the father of lies by research or reason, you overcome him by revelation. In the high priestly prayer, Jesus petitioned our heavenly Father on our behalf:

> I am coming to you now, but I say these things while I am still in the world, so that they may have the full measure of my joy within them. I have given them your word and the world has hated them, for they are not of the world any more than I am of the world. My prayer is not that you take them out of the world but that you protect them from the evil one. They are not of the world, even as I am not of it. Sanctify them by the truth; your word is truth (John 17:13-17, *NIV*).

God is not going to remove us from the negativity of this fallen world. Yet we are sanctified and protected by the truth of God's Word. Jesus said, "I have told you these things, so that in me you may have peace. In this world you will have trouble. But take heart! I have overcome the world" (John 16:33, *NIV*). Renewing our mind with truth will not continue if we don't actively work to sustain it. David said, "I will meditate on Your precepts and regard Your ways. I shall delight in Your statutes; I shall not forget Your word" (Ps. 119:15-16). Every mental stronghold that is torn down in Christ makes the next one easier to tear down. Every thought we take captive makes the next one more likely to surrender. Lifestyle depression is the result of repeated blows that come from living in a fallen world. Rehearsing the truth again and again is the key to renewing our mind.

4. Commit Yourself to Good Behavior

Philippians 4:9

We are not instantly delivered from lifestyle depression; we have to grow out of it. It takes time to renew our mind, but it doesn't take time to change our behavior, which facilitates the process of renewing our mind, as well as positively affecting how we feel. When Cain and Abel brought their offerings to the Lord, He was not pleased with Cain's offering: "So Cain became very angry and his countenance fell. Then the LORD said to Cain, 'Why are you angry? And why has your countenance fallen? If you do well, will not your countenance be lifted up? And if you do not do well, sin is crouching at the door; and its desire is for you, but you must master it'" (Gen. 4:5-7). In other words, we don't feel our way into good behavior, we behave our way into good feelings. If we wait until we feel like doing what is right, we will likely never do it. Jesus said, "Now that you know these things, you will be blessed if you do them" (John 13:17, *NIV*).

That is why some interventions for depression focus on behavior. Depressed people are helped by participating in activities that pull them out of their negative moods. Go to work even though you may not feel like getting out of bed. Plan an activity and stick to it. Get more physical exercise and commit yourself to follow through on your plans. You may *feel* tired, but your body needs exercise. Start with a low-impact aerobic program or take walks with friends and family members. Continue routine duties even though you feel like you don't have the energy. These behavioral interventions or activities are only a start in developing a healthy lifestyle. If these activities are too difficult or physically impossible, seek the kind of medical help that will get you back on your feet. Certain negative behaviors exist that will only contribute to depression. Drowning your sorrows with drugs and alcohol is at the top of this destructive list. People choose alcohol or drugs to medicate their pain and quiet their minds—a means of coping with the difficulties of life. Although this may bring temporary relief, it will only further contribute to the depression. To understand how living in an oppressive situation can result in depression and alcoholism, read Neil and Mike Quarles's book *Overcoming Addictive Behavior* (Regal Books, 2003).

5. SEEK MEANINGFUL RELATIONSHIPS
Hebrews 10:24-25

One of the major symptoms of depression is withdrawal from meaningful relationships. Isolating yourself and being alone with your negative thoughts will only contribute to the downward spiral. You may feel like you need to be alone, but you need to stay in contact with the right people. Wrong associations and relationships, however, will only pull you down: "Do not be misled: 'Bad company corrupts good character'" (1 Cor. 15:33, *NIV*). We suggest that you see your pastor or find a godly pastor or counselor in your community. Tell him or her your struggle with depression, and ask him or her what they offer in terms of fellowship. A good church will have many meaningful activities and small discipleship groups in which you can get the prayer and care that you need.

Anybody who has suffered from a lifestyle depression for any length of time will have one or more people who they need to forgive and some with whom they need to be reconciled. Most of these issues will be resolved during the Steps. Concerning the need to seek the forgiveness of others, Jesus said, "If you are offering your gift at the altar and there remember that your brother has something against you, leave your gift there in front of the altar. First go and be reconciled to your brother; then come and offer your gift" (Matt. 5:23-24, *NIV*). If you need to forgive someone, go to God; but if you have offended or hurt someone, then don't go to church, go to that person and be reconciled. You will have little mental peace if you don't.

6. Overcome Your Losses
Philippians 4:8

Reactive depression is different from lifestyle depression because some specific event or loss triggered it. A loss can be real, threatened or imagined. An imagined loss is often a negative thought (lie) that is believed. Recall that Elijah's downward spiral began when he believed a lie and feared Jezebel more than God (see chapter 6). Everyone is going to experience losses. How we handle any crisis will determine how fast we recover from the loss and how well we conform to the image of God. The following steps will help you overcome your losses.[4]

Identify Each Loss
Most losses are easy to recognize, but some aren't. Changing jobs or moving to a new location can precipitate a depression. Even though both could improve a person's social status and financial base, something may be lost in the transition. The attachment could be to family, church, friends and familiar places. Many losses are multifaceted. For instance, the loss of a job could also include the loss of wages, social status, respect and so on.

People don't react the same to losses because they have different values and different maturity levels. In order to get beyond denial and continue with the grieving process, people must understand what it is that they are losing or have already lost. People can be depressed because they didn't get the job they hoped for or the promotion they wanted. Some have planned their life to go a certain way, and now their dreams for the future have been dashed.

Separate the Concrete from the Abstract Losses

Concrete losses can be seen, touched, measured and defined. Abstract losses refer to personal goals, dreams and ideas. Overcoming concrete losses is usually easier, because they are more definable. They vary from losing a card game to losing a leg. Most wouldn't be very depressed over losing a card game, but if you were representing the United States in the world bridge championships and you lost the final game, it could be very depressing. Abstract losses relate deeply to who we are and why we are here. Many concrete losses, such as the loss of a job, are contaminated with abstract losses. You may find a new job next week but remain depressed because you feel the pain of rejection and wrongly believe you are a failure. That is another reason why it is so important to understand who we are in Christ and find our acceptance, security and significance in Him.

Separate Real, Imagined and Threatened Losses

You cannot process an imagined or threatened loss in the same way you can a real loss. In a real loss you can face the truth, grieve the loss and make the necessary changes that make it possible to go on living in a meaningful way.

Convert Imagined and Threatened Losses to Real Losses

Imagined losses are distortions of reality. They are based on suspicions or lies that we believe or presumptions that we make. The mind will assume certain things when we don't know the facts. Seldom does the mind assume the best. We don't always act on our assumptions; but if we do, we shall be counted among the fools, because through presumption comes nothing but strife (see Prov. 13:10). People ruminate various possibilities and consequences in their minds until they are depressed. Instead, verify assumptions and then follow Peter's advice:

> Cast all your anxiety on him because he cares for you. Be self-controlled and alert. Your enemy the devil prowls around like a roaring lion looking for someone to devour. Resist him, standing firm in the faith (1 Pet. 5:7-8, *NIV*).

Threatened losses have the potential of being real losses. They include such things as the possibility of a layoff at work or a spouse who threatens to leave. Such threats can precipitate a depression, but since there is at the present time no finality to the loss, it cannot be processed. It is helpful for us to think what the worst-case scenario may be and then ask ourselves, *Can we live with it?* This prepares us for impermanence. We all face potential losses. No one has the right to determine who we are, and no one can keep us from being the person God created us to be. Therefore, when someone threatens you, respond the way Peter advises:

> Who is going to harm you if you are eager to do good? But even if you should suffer for what is right, you are blessed. "Do not fear what they fear; do not be frightened." But in your hearts set apart Christ as Lord. Always be prepared to give an answer to everyone who asks you to give the reason for the hope that you have. But do this with gentleness and respect, keeping a clear conscience, so that those who speak maliciously against your good behavior in Christ may be ashamed of their slander. It is

better, if it is God's will, to suffer for doing good than for doing evil (1 Pet. 3:13-17, *NIV*).

These are growth issues, not terminal ones, if you understand life from an eternal perspective. What is the worst thing that could happen to you? You could die. But is that intolerable? Paul said, "For to me, to live is Christ and to die is gain" (Phil. 1:21). Put anything else in the formula and the result is loss. *For me to live is my health; then to die would be loss. For me to live is my family; then to die would be loss.* This is not a license to commit suicide; it is a liberating truth that allows us to live a responsible life. The person who is free from the fear of death is free to live responsibly today.

Facilitate the Grieving Process

The natural response to any crisis is to deny that it is really happening, get angry that it did happen and then try to alter the situation by bargaining with God or others. When that doesn't work, you feel depressed. You cannot bypass the grieving process, but you can shorten it by allowing yourself to feel the full force of the loss. The fact that certain losses are depressing is reality. It hurts to lose something that has value to you. You cannot fully process your loss until you feel its full force. Jesus probably had that in mind when He said, "Blessed are those who mourn, for they shall be comforted" (Matt. 5:4).

Face the Reality of the Loss

Only after you have faced the full impact of the loss are you ready to deal with the reality of the loss. This is the critical juncture. Are you going to resign from life, succumb to the depression and drop out, or are you going to accept what you cannot change and let go of the loss? You can feel sorry for yourself for the rest of your life, or you can decide to live with your loss and learn how to go on in a meaningful way.

Develop a Biblical Perspective on the Loss

The trials and tribulations of life are intended to produce proven character. We suffer for the sake of righteousness. We can potentially come through any crisis a better person than the person we were before. Losses are inevitable. They are not intended to destroy us, but they will reveal who we are. People have discovered the truth of who they are in Christ as a direct result of losses. Each subsequent loss only deepens that reality, perfects our characters and prepares us for an even greater ministry.

Renew Your Mind to the Truth of Who You Really Are in Christ

We are all going to be victimized by losses and abuses. We can drown in our sorrow, blame others, claim that life is unfair and stay depressed the rest of our lives. Whether we remain a victim is our choice. We are not just products of our pasts; we are new creations in Christ. Nothing nor anybody can keep us from being the person God created us to be. Like the apostle Paul, we count everything but loss apart from the surpassing value of knowing Christ Jesus our Lord: "For we who live are constantly being delivered over to death for Jesus' sake, so that the life of Jesus also may be manifested in our mortal flesh" (2 Cor. 4:11).

7. LET IT GO

Ephesians 4:31-32

A woman shared that her best friend ran off with her husband 10 years earlier. She was deeply hurt by this incredible betrayal and disloyalty. She thought her life was ruined by those adulterers, and there was nothing she could do about it. For 10 years she smoldered in bitterness and depression. Feelings of resentment and plots of revenge ruminated in her mind. Neil told her,

"I see you with one fist extended up to heaven where God has a firm grip on you. Your other fist is hanging onto your past and you aren't about to let go. You are not even hanging on to God,

> LET GO OF YOUR PAST AND
> GRAB HOLD OF GOD. IT IS
> YOUR ONLY HOPE.

but your heavenly Father is hanging on to you, His beloved child. Isn't it time to let it go? You are only hurting yourself." At the end of the conference, she worked through *The Steps to Freedom in Christ*, and she let it go. The next morning she sang in the choir with a countenance that portrayed a liberated child of God.

Let go of your past and grab hold of God. It is your only hope. May these closing thoughts help you do just that:

Once I held in my tightly clinched fist . . . ashes. Ashes from a burn inflicted upon my 10-year-old body. Ashes I didn't ask for. The scar was forced on me. And for 17 years the fire smoldered. I kept my fist closed in secret, hating those ashes, yet unwilling to release them. Not sure if I could. Not convinced it was worth it. Marring the things I touched and leaving black marks everywhere . . . or so it seemed. I tried to undo it all, but the marks were always there to remind me that I couldn't. I really couldn't. But God could! His sweet Holy Spirit spoke to my heart one night in tearful desperation. He whispered, "I want to give you beauty for your ashes, the oil of joy for your mourning and the garment of praise for your spirit of heaviness." I had never heard of such a trade as this: Beauty? Beauty for ashes? My sadly stained memory for His healing Word? My soot-like dreams for His songs in the night? My helpless and hurting emotions for His ever-constant peace?

How could I be so stubborn as to refuse an offer such as this? So willingly, yet in slow motion, and yes, while sobbing, I opened my bent fingers and let the ashes drop to the ground. In silence, I heard the wind blow them away. Away from me . . . forever. I am now able to place my open hands gently around the fist of another hurting soul and say with confidence, "Let them go. There really is beauty beyond your comprehension. Go ahead—trust Him. His beauty for your ashes."[5]

IN CHRIST

I AM ACCEPTED IN CHRIST

John 1:12	I am God's child.
John 15:15	I am Christ's friend.
Romans 5:1	I have been justified.
1 Corinthians 6:17	I am united with the Lord, and I am one with Him in spirit.
1 Corinthians 6:19-20	I have been bought with a price. I belong to God.
1 Corinthians 12:27	I am a member of Christ's Body.
Ephesians 1:1	I am a saint.
Ephesians 1:5	I have been adopted as God's child.
Ephesians 2:18	I have direct access to God through the Holy Spirit.
Colossians 1:14	I have been redeemed and forgiven of all my sins.
Colossians 2:10	I am complete in Christ.

I AM SECURE IN CHRIST

Romans 8:1-2	I am free from condemnation.
Romans 8:28	I am assured that all things work together for good.
Romans 8:31-34	I am free from any condemning charges against me.
Romans 8:35-39	I cannot be separated from the love of God.
2 Corinthians 1:21-22	I have been established, anointed and sealed by God.
Philippians 1:6	I am confident that the good work God has begun in me will be perfected.
Philippians 3:20	I am a citizen of heaven.
Colossians 3:3	I am hidden with Christ in God.
2 Timothy 1:7	I have not been given a spirit of fear but of power, love and a sound mind.
Hebrews 4:16	I can find grace and mercy to help in times of need.
1 John 5:18	I am born of God and the evil one cannot touch me.

I AM SIGNIFICANT IN CHRIST

Matthew 5:13-14	I am the salt and light of the earth.
John 15:1,5	I am a branch of the true vine, a channel of His life.
John 15:16	I have been chosen and appointed to bear fruit.
Acts 1:8	I am a personal witness of Christ.
1 Corinthians 3:16	I am God's temple.
2 Corinthians 5:17-21	I am a minister of reconciliation for God.
2 Corinthians 6:1	I am God's coworker.
Ephesians 2:6	I am seated with Christ in the heavenly realm.
Ephesians 2:10	I am God's workmanship.
Ephesians 3:12	I may approach God with freedom and confidence.
Philippians 4:13	I can do all things through Christ who strengthens me.

THE OVERCOMER'S COVENANT IN CHRIST

1. I place all my trust and confidence in the Lord, and I put no confidence in the flesh. I declare myself to be dependent on God.

2. I consciously and deliberately choose to submit to God and resist the devil by denying myself, picking up my cross daily and following Jesus.

3. I choose to humble myself before the mighty hand of God in order that He may exalt me at the proper time.

4. I declare the truth that I am dead to sin—freed from it—and alive to God in Christ Jesus, since I have died with Christ and was raised with Him.

5. I gladly embrace the truth that I am now a child of God who is unconditionally loved and accepted. I reject the lie that I have to perform to be accepted, and I reject my fallen and natural identity that was derived from the world.

6. I declare that sin shall no longer be master over me, because I am not under the Law. I am under grace, and there is no more guilt or condemnation because I am spiritually alive in Christ Jesus.

7. I renounce every unrighteous use of my body, and I commit myself to no longer be conformed to this world but to be transformed by the renewing of my mind. I choose to believe the truth and walk in it, regardless of my feelings or circumstances.

8. I commit myself to take every thought captive to the obedience of Christ and choose to think upon that which is true, honorable, right, pure and lovely.

9. I commit myself to God's great goal for my life—to conform to His image. I know that I will face many trials, but God has given me the victory. I am not a victim but an overcomer in Christ.

10. I choose to adopt the attitude of Christ, which is to do nothing from selfishness or empty conceit but with humility of mind. I will regard others as more important than myself, and I will look out not only for my own personal interests but also the interests of others. I know that it is more blessed to give than to receive.

ENDNOTES

Introduction

1. It is a well-established fact that people become physically sick because of mental, emotional and spiritual reasons. The minimum estimate is 50 percent, and you will hear as high as 75 percent, of illness is psychosomatic. At least 25 percent of the "healings" in the Gospels are actually deliverances from evil spirits.
2. "Depression," *National Insitutes of Mental Health*. http://www.nimh.nih.gov/publicat/depression.cfm#intro (accessed March 24, 2003).
3. Michael Burlingame, *The Inner World of Abraham Lincoln* (Urbana, IL: University of Illinois Press, 1994), n.p.
4. Ibid., p. 40.
5. Ibid., p. 100.
6. Anthony Storr, *Churchill's Black Dog, Kafka's Mice, and Other Phenomena of the Human Mind* (New York: Grove Press, 1988), n.p.
7. Source unknown.

Chapter One

1. *Denver Post*, February 18, 1998, p. 106.
2. Source unknown.
3. John Gray, *Men Are from Mars, Women Are from Venus* (New York: Harper Collins Publishers, 1992), pp. 30-35.

Chapter Two

1. David Burns, M.D., *The Feeling Good Handbook* (New York: Plime, 1989), p. 59.
2. Demitri and Janice Papolos, *Overcoming Depression* (New York: Harper Perennial, 1992), p. 7.
3. Kay Redfield Jamison, *Touched with Fire* (New York: Free Press Paperbacks, 1993).
4. Kay Redfield Jamison, *An Unquiet Mind* (New York: Vintage Books, 1995).
5. Leo Tolstoy, *Confessions* (New York: W. W. Norton, 1983), pp. 28-29.
6. Source unknown.
7. Michael Lemonick, "The Mood Molecule," *Time*, no. 29 (September 1997), p. 75.
8. *Time* (September 29, 1997), p. 76.
9. Medical information compiled in conjunction with Lyle Torguson, M.D., and Stephen King, M.D.

10. Thomas J. Moore, *Prescription for Disaster* (New York: Simon and Schuster, 1998), p. 115.
11. D. A. Kessler, "Introducing MedWatch," *Journal of the American Medical Association*, vol. 269 (1993), pp. 2765-2768.
12. Mitch and Susan Golant, *What to Do When Someone You Love Is Depressed* (New York: Villard Books, 1996), p. 10.
13. Ibid., p. 11.
14. Martin Seligman, *Learned Optimism* (New York: Pocket Books, 1990), pp. 65-66.

Chapter Three

1. *The Steps to Freedom in Christ* is a tool to help people resolve personal and spiritual conflicts through repentance and faith in God. It can be purchased from Freedom in Christ Ministries or any Christian bookstore. The theology and methodology are explained in Neil T. Anderson, *Discipleship Counseling* (Regal Books, 2003).
2. Demitri and Janice Papolos, *Overcoming Depression* (New York: Harper Perennial, 1992), pp. 88-89.
3. For more information, see William Backus, *Telling Yourself the Truth* (Bethany Fellowship, 1980), and David Stoop, *Self Talk: Key to Personal Growth* (Fleming H. Revell, 1982).

Chapter Four

1. Anne Olivier Bell and Andrew McNeillie, eds., *The Diary of Virginia Woolf* (New York: Harcourt, Brace, Jovanovich, 1984), p. 226.
2. Gary R. Collins, *Christian Counseling: A Comprehensive Guide* (Dallas, TX: Word Publishing, 1988), p. 318.
3. Neil T. Anderson and Charles Mylander, *The Christ-Centered Marriage: Discovering and Enjoying Your Freedom in Christ Together* (Ventura, CA: Regal Books, 1996), p. 108.
4. George Barna, *The Frog in the Kettle* (Ventura, CA: Regal Books, 1990), p. 229; for further clarification, see Neil T. Anderson and David Park, *Overcoming a Negative Self-Image* (Regal Books, 2003).
5. David Meyers in *Psychology and Christianity*, eds. Eric L. Johnson and Stanton L. Jones (Downers Grove, IL: InterVarsity Press, 2000), pp. 62-63.

Chapter Five

1. Frank Mead, *The Encyclopedia of Religious Quotations* (Westwood, NJ: Fleming H. Revell, 1965), p. 234.
2. Sherwood Wirt and Kersten Beckstrom, eds., *Living Quotations for Christians* (New York: Harper and Row, 1974), p. 114.

3. Frank Minirth et al., *How to Beat Burnout* (Chicago: Moody Press, 1986), p. 135.
4. George Sweeting, comp., *Great Quotes and Illustrations* (Waco, TX: Word Books, 1985), p. 143.

Chapter Six
1. Demitri and Janice Papolos, *Overcoming Depression* (New York: Harper Perennial, 1992), p. 89.
2. To help you set up scriptural boundaries to protect yourself from further abuse, we recommend Henry Cloud and John Townsend, *Boundaries* (Zondervan Publishing House, 2002).
3. Source unknown.
4. Neil T. Anderson, *Victory over the Darkness* (Ventura, CA: Regal Books, 2000), p. 115.

Chapter Seven
1. Source unknown.
2. Martin Seligman, *Learned Optimism* (New York: Pocket Books, 1990), pp. 65-66.
3. Joni Eareckson Tada (Focus on the Family radio, June 1993).
4. Jim Elliot, *The Journals of Jim Elliot*, Elisabeth Elliot, ed. (Grand Rapids, MI: Fleming H. Revell, 1978), p. 174.
5. Dr. Reinhold Niebuhr, "Serenity Prayer."
6. Edwin E. Aldrin, *Return to Earth* (New York: Random House, 1973), quoted in *Current Biographic Yearbook*, 1993.

Chapter Eight
1. J. I. Packer, *Rediscovering Holiness* (Ann Arbor, MI: Vine Books, 1992), p. 250.
2. Gordon R. Lewis, "Suffering and Anguish," *Zondervan Pictorial Encyclopedia of the Bible*, ed. Merrill C. Tenny (Grand Rapids, MI: Zondervan Publishing House, 1976).
3. C. S. Lewis, *The Problem of Pain* (New York: Macmillan, 1962), p. 93.
4. John Freccero, *Dante: The Poetics of Conversion*, ed. Rachel Jacoff (Cambridge, MA: Harvard University Press, 1986), p. 70.
5. Lewis, *The Problem of Pain*, p. 91.
6. Source unknown.
7. C. S. Lewis, *The Joyful Christian: 127 Readings from C. S. Lewis* (New York: Macmillan, 1977), p. 210.
8. H. W. Robinson, *Suffering: Human and Divine* (New York: Macmillan, 1939), p. 139.
9. Lewis, *The Problem of Pain*, p. 93.
10. Peter Kreeft, *Making Sense out of Suffering* (Ann Arbor, MI: Servant Books, 1986), p. 78.

11. Philip Edgcumbe Hughes, *Paul's Second Epistle to the Corinthians* (Grand Rapids, MI: Eerdmans Publishing Co., 1962), p. 11.

Chapter Nine
1. E. Stanley Jones, quoted in Sherwood Wirt and Kersten Beckstrom, eds., *Living Quotations for Christians* (New York: Harper and Row, 1974), p. 35.
2. Archibald Hart, *Counseling the Depressed* (Waco, TX: Word Books, 1987), p. 99.
3. Daniel Goleman, *Emotional Intelligence,* quoted in Mitch and Susan Golant, *What to Do When Someone You Love Is Depressed* (New York: Villard Books, 1996), p. 23.
4. We want to thank Archibald Hart for the insights in his book *Counseling the Depressed* (Waco, TX: Word Books, 1987), pp. 133-143.
5. Source unknown.

BOOKS AND RESOURCES BY
DR. NEIL T. ANDERSON

CORE MESSAGE AND MATERIALS

The Bondage Breaker and study guide and audiobook (Harvest House Publishers, 2000)—with well over 1 million copies in print, this book explains spiritual warfare, what our protection is, ways that we are vulnerable and how we can live a liberated life in Christ.

Breaking Through to Spiritual Maturity (Regal Books, 2000)—this curriculum teaches the basic message of Freedom in Christ Ministries.

Discipleship Counseling and videocassettes (Regal Books, 2003)—combines the concepts of discipleship and counseling, and the practical integration of theology and psychology, for helping Christians resolve their personal and spiritual conflicts through repentance.

The Steps to Freedom in Christ and interactive videocassette (Regal Books, 2000)—this discipleship counseling tool helps Christians resolve their personal and spiritual conflicts.

Victory over the Darkness and study guide, audiobook and videocassettes (Regal Books, 2000)—with well over 1 million copies in print, this core book explains who you are in Christ, how you walk by faith, how your mind and emotions function and how to relate to one another in Christ.

SPECIALIZED BOOKS

The Biblical Guide to Alternative Medicine with Dr. Michael Jacobson (Regal Books, 2003)—develops a grid by which you can evaluate medical practices. It applies the grid to the world's most recognized philosophies of medicine and health.

Blessed Are the Peacemakers with Dr. Charles Mylander (Regal Books, 2002)—explains the ministry of reconciliation and gives practical steps for being reconciled with others.

Breaking the Bondage of Legalism with Rich Miller and Paul Travis (Harvest House Publishers, 2003)—an exposure and explanation of legalism and how to overcome it.

The Christ-Centered Marriage with Dr. Charles Mylander (Regal Books, 1997)—explains God's divine plan for marriage and the steps that couples can take to resolve their difficulties.

Christ-Centered Therapy with Dr. Terry and Julianne Zuehlke (Zondervan Publishing House, 2000)—a textbook explaining the practical integration of theology and psychology for professional counselors.

Daily in Christ with Joanne Anderson (Harvest House Publishers, 2000)—this popular daily devotional is being used by thousands of Internet subscribers every day.

Finding Hope Again with Hal Baumchen (Regal Books, 1999)—explains depression and how to overcome it.

Freedom from Addiction with Mike and Julia Quarles (Regal Books, 1997)—using Mike's testimony, this book explains the nature of chemical addictions and how to overcome them in Christ.

Freedom from Fear with Rich Miller (Harvest House Publishers, 1999)—explains fear, anxiety and disorders, and how to overcome them.

Freedom in Christ Bible (Zondervan Publishing House, 2002)—a one-year discipleship study with notes in the Bible.

Getting Anger Under Control with Rich Miller (Harvest House Publishers, 1999)—explains the basis for anger and how to control it.

God's Power at Work in You with Dr. Robert L. Saucy (Harvest House Publishers, 2001)—a thorough analysis of sanctification and practical instruction on how we grow in Christ.

Leading Teens to Freedom in Christ with Rich Miller (Regal Books, 1997)—this discipleship counseling book focuses on teenagers, their problems and how to solve them.

One Day at a Time with Mike and Julia Quarles (Regal Books, 2000)—this devotional helps those who struggle with addictive behaviors and how to discover the grace of God on a daily basis.

Released from Bondage with Dr. Fernando Garzon and Judith E. King (Thomas Nelson, 2002)—contains personal accounts of bondage with explanatory notes showing how people found their freedom in Christ, and how the message of Freedom in Christ can be applied to therapy with research results.

The Seduction of Our Children with Steve Russo (Harvest House Publishers, 1991)—explains what teenagers are experiencing and how parents can be equipped to help them.

Setting Your Church Free with Dr. Charles Mylander (Regal Books, 1994)—this book on Christian leadership also explains corporate bondage and how it can be resolved in Christ.

The Spiritual Protection of Our Children with Peter and Sue Vander Hook (Regal Books, 1996)—using the Vander Hook's experience, this book explains how parents can help their children.

A Way of Escape with Russ Rummer (Harvest House Publishers, 1998)—explains sexual strongholds and how they can be torn down in Christ.

Who I Am in Christ (Regal Books, 2001)—describes in 36 short chapters who you are in Christ and how He meets your deepest needs.

VICTORY OVER THE DARKNESS SERIES

Overcoming Negative Self-Image with Dave Park (Regal Books, 2003)
Overcoming Addictive Behavior with Mike Quarles (Regal Books, 2003)
Overcoming Depression with Joanne Anderson (Regal Books, 2004)
Overcoming Doubt (Regal Books, 2004)

THE BONDAGE BREAKER SERIES

Finding Freedom in a Sex-Obsessed World (Harvest House Publishers, 2004)

Finding God's Will in Spiritually Deceptive Times (Harvest House Publishers, 2003)

Praying by the Power of the Spirit (Harvest House Publishers, 2003)

YOUTH BOOKS

Awesome God with Rich Miller (Harvest House Publishers, 1996)

The Bondage Breaker—Youth Edition with Dave Park (Harvest House Publishers, 2001)

Extreme Faith with Dave Park (Harvest House Publishers, 1996)

Higher Ground with Dave Park and Dr. Robert L. Saucy (1999)[*]

Purity Under Pressure with Dave Park (Harvest House Publishers, 1995)

Radical Image with Dave Park and Dr. Robert L. Saucy (Harvest House Publishers, 1998)[*]

Real Life with Dave Park (Harvest House Publishers, 2000)[*]

Reality Check with Rich Miller (Harvest House Publishers, 1996)

Righteous Pursuit with Dave Park (Harvest House Publishers, 2000)

Stomping Out Depression with Dave Park (Regal Books, 2001)

Stomping Out Fear with Rich Miller and Dave Park (Harvest House Publishers, 2003)

Stomping Out the Darkness with Dave Park (Regal Books, 1999)

Ultimate Love with Dave Park (Harvest House Publishers, 1996)

[*] Available from Freedom in Christ Ministries only